RED'S REVENGE (SPECIAL EDITION)

RED'S REVENGE (SPECIAL EDITION)

SUMMER N DAWN

Contents

TRIGGER WARNINGS ... ix
Dedication ... x

Part One ... 1
   I Roman ... 3
   II Roman ... 15
   III Red (Asia) ... 23
   IV Red ... 31
   V Roman ... 35
   VI Red ... 43
   VII Roman ... 47
   VIII Roman ... 53
   IX Red ... 57
   X Red ... 63
   XI Roman ... 69
   XII Red ... 75
   XIII Roman ... 81

XIV	Red	89
XV	Roman	99
XVI	Red	103
XVII	Red	111
XVIII	Roman	115
Part Two		117
XIX	Red	119
XX	Kass	121
XXI	Red	125
XXII	Kass	129
XXIII	Red	133
XXIV	Kass	137
XXV	S	139
XXVI	Red	141
XXVII	Kass	147
XXVIII	Red	151
XXIX	Kass	155
Part Three		157
XXX	Roman	159
XXXI	Red	163
XXXII	S	165
XXXIII	Red	167
XXXIV	Sasha	171
XXXV	Red	173
XXXVI	Kass	175

XXXVII	Roman	179
XXXVIII	Kass	183
XXXIX	Roman	185
XL	Red	189
XLI	Roman	193
XLII	Red	195
XLIII	Roman	197
XLIV	Kass	199
XLV	Red	201
XLVI	Roman	203
XLVII	Red	205
XLVIII	Roman	207
XLIX	Red	209
L	Roman	213
LI	Red	215
LII	Roman	217
LIII	Red	221

Notes 227
Notes 229
About the Author 231

Copyright © 2024 by Summer N Dawn LLC
Cover by Book Degins by Shae
All rights reserved. No part of this book may be reproduced in any manner whatsoever without written permission except in the case of brief quotations embodied in critical articles and reviews.
First Printing, 2024

TRIGGER WARNINGS

This novel contains the following:

VIOLENCE

BLOOD

PROFANITY

SEX

SEX TRAFFICKING

RAPE

TORTURE

EMOTIONAL ABUSE

TALK OF PREGNANCY

PREGNANCY

If you are triggered by the above, please REFRAIN from reading! Your mental health comes first!

TO MY SUNSHINE, YOU NEVER LET MY LIGHT DIM. YOU DIDN'T LET MY DARKNESS SWAY YOUR LOVE.

TO MY BOOKISH BADDIES AND ENCHANTED READERS, BE YOUR OWN STRENGTH AND NEVER WAIVER! YOU HAVE GIVEN ME STRENGTH, SO LET ME ENTERTAIN YOU!

TO E. LYNN, MAY YOUR JOURNEY BE LONG AND PROSPEROUS! YOUR SUPPORT AND ADVICE ARE GOLDEN!

Part One

I

Roman

The last two months have been a whirlwind.

My sister is now married and can boss me around again. Kassani is now married to Massimo, Don of the Ballentine Bratva and my boss.

My sister and I haven't always had the most leisurely life, but as long as we stuck together, we always made it through. It is beautiful how life brings us back together. She got the love she deserves.

She is loved, protected, catered to, and never wants anything.

I have never wanted to be in love, but seeing how happy Kass is makes me want to try.

My relationships consist of casual flings. I have only had one serious relationship in the last five years; her name was Renee Rosenthal.

I fell hard and fast for Renee. We were together for three and a half years. We were ready to walk down the aisle, but I discovered she was not on the market.

She was already married. She was married to Vito Vincent, a rival of the Ballentine Bratva; we were all fooled. She had gone through intense plastic surgery. Records show she had $525,000 worth of plastic surgery. We tried to find the exact breakdown of the procedures she had done. But we know for sure she had a nose job, breast lift, breast implants, and a butt lift. Never did I imagine a plastic Barbie would dupe me.

After everything with Renee, I have lost trust in all women except Kass.

Kass is the only woman who I know would never harm me.

Renee filmed our entire sex life and sent it to her husband.

Vincent's inadequate army viewed all the moments that I thought were intimate and sacred between us. Vincent and his men can not be considered Bratva; only one hundred existed. I felt violated and betrayed. Vincent and Renee both received everything they deserved.

I had invested time, money, and love into Renee. I spent $10,000 on a custom engagement ring, all for her to laugh in my face and throw my "cheap" engagement ring into the ocean. Luckily, I was able to retrieve it and get my money back.

If it were up to me, Renee would be at the bottom of the ocean, in the exact spot where she threw my ring. But instead, she and her precious husband are covered in Rumble and ash, burnt to a crisp. Vincent and his men are laid to Rest in the same spot. It all came to an end with Marcus and his indestructible plan. No one will wonder or ever hear about Vincent's Army.

If I could find love like Kass and Massimo, my life would be complete. My sister has always felt like a burden to everyone who cares for her.

Kass has never burdened Kiera and me. Kiera loves Kass like a baby sister, even though they are the same age. Nothing can tear Kass and Kiera apart. Kiera has a love just as great. She is married to Marcus, Massimo's right-hand man. She is treated like she walks on water. She can do no wrong in Marcus 'eyes, not that she ever would. Kiera is a Saint, although her life has been as rough as mine and Kass's.

Kiera is Kass protector and sister. The day Kass married Massimo, Kiera had her childhood wish granted. She and Kass were married at the same time. Kass and the boys planned it so that Kay and Key would always share the same birthday and now the exact wedding anniversary. They have a bond that no one can take away from them, and with their powerful husbands in their arms, nothing stands in their way.

I need a strong woman by my side.

I have a woman in mind but am afraid to trust again. Asia Hope Levine knows all about Bratva's life. She is the head spy for our group. She is strong, independent, and dangerous. Her kill count is up there with Massimo's.

Does she scare me? Not all of her strength, not all of her independence. The only thing about her that scares me is her gender. After Renee, I am scared to have feelings, afraid to love a woman. Not all women are vicious, but what if I fall hard again? What if I am duped again? What would my Bratva brothers think of me?

It never seemed like a long time without a woman's touch. I dumped all my casual flings because I was tired of them wanting more. I couldn't see any of them fitting in with Kass and Kiera. If they don't vibe with Kay and Key, the answer is goodbye.

Asia

It's days like this I dread, days I have to rescue women from a sex ring. One day, this will end; I will end it. I used to be one of them. I was captured in 2019, and at first gave up. I let my circumstances get the best of me; I let over twenty men use and abuse me.

I still have a few physical scars that won't disappear. One of them keeps me from showing skin; I was sliced open from my armpit to my hip. The thick scar line makes it hard to hide the entire side of my body. The only skin I show now is my arms and chest, and I will not allow the world to see me as vulnerable.

I am not the scared little girl I once was; now, I am the head spy for the Ballentine Bratva.

Would I ever consider a different line of work? Not until the world is safe from all the perverted sex trafficking. I will soon end the person who sold me my first ring. I trusted her; Shelia was my adoptive mom. Shelia Barnes adopted me when I was fourteen; little did I know she was grooming me for the future.

She taught me everything, including how to do my makeup, hair, and flirt. She coached me through my first kiss, the first red flag.

She made sure she was there when we were ready to kiss. She had adjustments she wanted me to make every step of the way. She ensured my arms were around his neck, and I knew all the proper edicts.

My biological parents gave me up when I was just three days old. At first, Sheila seemed like a caring and loving foster mother. And as I grew and my body started to develop, she saw a potential money maker, not a child. She taught me everything she could so I could make her the best money I could. Never in my wildest dreams did I think I would be sold to a sex trafficking ring.

The first time I was sold, I was brought back to Sheila because the person who bought me had morals. He said I wasn't of age and that he would go to jail for a lot of things, but defiling a minor was not one of them. The second time I was sold was not as easy. After the first time, Sheila got smart.

She kept me hidden away until I came of age. She had documents drawn up saying that I could not take care of myself. At the age of 21, she was still in charge of me. While locked away, I learned all I could about Sheila and her plans. Not only did she plan to sell me, but she planned to hide the money away so I would never touch it. The second time I was sold, I was sold to an older gentleman. He can't even be classified as a gentleman; he didn't make me into what he wanted me to be. He made me a people pleaser. He knew his clients and their wants, so he ensured that I fit in that mold.

I was taught to obey and never question what any man does to me. I was taught that my feelings don't matter and that my pleasure is only allowed if my buyer allows it. I was taught that I am a piece of flesh, a piece of flesh that cannot be loved. I'm a piece of flesh that should only do what they're told and not speak unless spoken to. Not once when I was in captivity with these monsters did I ever show emotion.

I vowed that if I were rescued, I would make it my life's mission to protect women who get put in the trafficker's hands. I fulfill that vow daily by working for Massimo as his undercover spy in all the rings. Massimo and Roman rescued me three years ago. I was barely alive, and I let anyone use and abuse me. They rescued me a few days after Warren Corso slit me from armpit to hip, all for refusing to please him while he forced his twelve-year-old daughter to watch. There was no way I would subject that little girl to having that image burned into her head.

When they found me, I was almost dead; I only remember coming to when Roman was carrying me out of the makeshift brothel. I remember what he said that day, and I'll never forget it.

"Never let anyone dim your light; karma will make these monsters pay."

It took me a long time to realize what he meant. He meant that no matter what comes your way, stay true to yourself, and karma will take care of the rest.

Since the day I was rescued, I have vowed to be karma. I will not let a single trafficker escape, not because of what they did to me, but what they could potentially do to other women. Never in my life did I think killing monsters would bring me joy, but after enduring wickedness at the hands of someone I thought loved me, I will never stop until the world is free.

I may not be worthy of love, but that will not stop me from giving in to my desires. I desire to be held at night when I need it and spoiled with flowers and chocolates. I don't ask for much, and I know I don't deserve it, but the small part of me wants a small slice of being wanted and substantial.

I recently entered a casual fling, even though I shouldn't have done that. But he knows the risk and the life: Roman Hart. He's a strong man with a history of being a playboy.

If I wanted to be protected, I'm sure he would be up to the task, but that's not what I need. I need someone who is not going to want a lovey-dovey relationship.

I have known Roman for years; his sister is married to our Don now. Roman never lets anything stand in his way. I know very little about the heartbreak that he experienced. For a while, it was the talk of the compound. But I can see he has grown from that vile circumstance. I feel bad because all I do is trick men, make them think I can obey their wishes, and give them what they want. When in reality, I'm only there to take their life and rescue the women who never deserved to be in the trafficking ring.

I'm supposed to meet up with Roman in a few hours. I know we're not in a relationship, but I don't want to wear my usual what I call uniform. Today I'm going to put on a skin-tight black T-shirt dress. Normally, I don't wear dresses, but he makes me feel some way. I don't know what I think, but maybe time will tell.

I decided to do very little makeup. On a typical day, I'm full of clown faces so everyone doesn't see the real me, and I can focus on the mission. But today, I'm going to be relaxed. We will eat and then meet up with the crew later. That's how we're able to go out together. Everyone knows we work together, and that's all they need to know.

I'm very private about my life. Of course, Massimo knows the truth. Roman only knows a little of it, and I plan to keep it that way. Learning about my past would make Roman shy away from me. I know I'm not like his ex, but I don't feel he needs all that drama.

We started this casual fling two months ago, right after Kass married. Massimo picked the right woman to marry. Kassani is a badass! Kass has been helping rescue and take care of some of the women from the sex rings. She has been training with them every day, teaching them self-defense and how to shoot. Kass comes from a humble background and has cerebral palsy. If anybody can teach someone to overcome and to be their best self, it's her.

The things I've heard men in the Bratva say about me make me think I might be a badass. But a small part of me knows I don't fit in that category. My baggage always brings me down. One day, I will find where I belong.

Jewelry or no jewelry? Jewelry! I will wear the red crystal necklace that Roman gave me a month after they rescued me. He knows I believe in crystals, but I don't think he's what red crystals mean. Red crystals mean love and passion but can also refer to earth and energy.

Did he know what I was lacking? Did he see the areas in which I struggle? Could he feel for me? Is he trying to tell me something?

Asia, get out of your head! He knows none of that! He probably thought it was a pretty color, so he got it for you.

I slip my feet into my red glitter flats. Comfortable footwear is my go-to. I am always prepared in case I have to chase someone down. But today, I chose my red flats to offset my black T-shirt dress and tied them to my red crystal necklace.

I'm feeling nice—not beautiful, but friendly. I feel like I could flirt a little with Roe. He wants to eat at Don's Bistro, a fitting name since Massimo owns it. It's not uncommon for our crew to eat there often, but it's also trendy here with locals and tourists, and we protect anyone who walks through our restaurant just in case anything occurs.

Let's do this; let's not think about work. Enjoy our time with Roe before it's back to business tomorrow. Let's flirt, let's eat, let's drink, and let's see whose place we end up at.

II

Roman

Don's is less busy than normally on a Friday afternoon.

There are more employee cars in the back than customer cars in the front, and only six customer vehicles in the front. Jared dropped me off even though I live two blocks from here. He was leaving the compound at the same time as me.

Today, I opted for a more respectable look. Kass bought me an outfit for my birthday last year; she said I needed a date outfit. It consists of designer black tailored pants that fit like they were made especially for me and a deep red button-down shirt that feels like the most excellent silk I have ever owned. Kass and Massimo picked out my shoes for this outfit, deep red loafers that match my shirt perfectly that an RH branded into them. These shoes are one of the most thoughtful gifts I have ever received.

Kass always makes my birthday unique, but Massimo helps her take the extra mile. Massimo will not tell my sister no, even when he should. Before this, Kass saved all her money because I mentioned I wanted a custom-made belt. She took notes and got it exactly how I wanted it. The belt is made with the finest quality leather, black leather. It is branded with an RH that matches my shoes but also has KC branded. She also had an A branded on the inside of the belt, but I can't figure out why. The best part of the belt is the custom laser-etched buckle; it has skulls and knives etched on the red buckle. From far away, it looks like a regular belt. You can't see the images unless your face is next to my pelvis.

Red is my favorite color. To me, red symbolizes power, hope, and direction. No matter what I wear, I have something red on me; most of the time, it's my belt.

Most recently, I got a tattoo. Nobody was with me, and I kept it a secret. My tattoo is a tribal sun in all-black ink except for the center. I had the artist fill the center with red ink, so even when I was not wearing red, I had red close to my heart.

I see her, a vision in black with red glittering shoes. She caresses her neck as she looks for me. How did I find her? Did she add red to her hair? Her hair shines bright red in the sun, and it looks like she put highlights on it. She looks like a glistening crystal heart; nothing can dim her sparkle.

Her eyes finally pierce mine, and as soon as they reach mine, it's like her eyes caught on fire.

She purrs, "Roe, what are you hungry for?"

Why do I feel like she is not talking about food? I am hungry for her.

"Hey Asia, maybe a steak or shrimp and some potatoes. What about you?"

Asia

We match! Kass let me help pick his outfit; he looks like I could eat him up! I didn't think he would wear the outfit; he would never know I helped with it. Kass even put an A on the inside of his belt. Kass believes Roe and I belong together, but that would only occur in a fiction novel.

Roe is too good for me; he is a Greek god that could make a girl cum just by licking his lips. This outfit makes me want to rip it off, throw it on the floor, and hold him hostage in my bed until morning. Maybe its the outfit, or maybe it's what he's hiding in his pants. I wonder if he's wearing the boxers I secretly picked out for him. I have to stop picturing his chiseled body naked, or I will not be able to eat. Well, I could have a long snack. A snack that could last at least 20 minutes or more. Our sex life is everything! I never leave famished.

After all the dark shit I have gone through sexually, Roe and sex flow like an ice-cold sprite sliding down your throat on a steamy day, especially when ice-cold water doesn't hit the spot. Roe can be vanilla or tangy; he lets me choose, depending on my hunger. I feel the anticipation building! I feel the hunger, the need to lick, the need to touch.

I clear my throat and mind, "Shrimp doesn't do it for me; maybe a juicy steak will satisfy my craving for now." I open the door and usher my Greek snack into Don's.

Let me get some sustenance in my body so he can fill me with his creamy yogurt.

We sit in our normal spot and Carrie comes to take our order.

"Good afternoon, you two! What will satisfy you today?" Carrie chirps.

I ordered for both of us: "Good afternoon! I'll have a juicy steak with a baked potato fully dressed, and Roe will have shrimp fettuccine with mashed potatoes. Oh, just water to drink, please, a pitcher!"

"You got it, sweet cheeks!" Carrie runs off to place our order.

Roe chuckles, "Sweet cheeks? I will call you that from now on since I know how sweet they really are."

Ummm, shit! What do I say to that? He's not talking about my mouth; my face turns beet red. I am pooling. This man knows me too intimately.

"Roe, hush! Someone could hear you."

Roman

This woman wants me to chain her to bed and turn her ass crimson. I have one rule: don't ever tell me to hush. She knows my rule but doesn't know why I have it.

I have been silenced all my life, so as an adult with a small amount of power, I will not be silenced ever again. My men know my rule as well. Only one person in my crew broke my rule; he can never break that rule again without a tongue.

I gave her a nickname that we only use in the bedroom. I whisper, "Red, you broke my rule. What should I do to you?"

Her breath catches, and the beet color of her face deepens. She crosses her legs and whispers, "Sunshine, I deserve to be spanked."

"Good girl, Red. Hard or soft?" I lick my lips.

Red leans forward, "The infraction was small, so the punishment should be soft. But Sunshine, you know how hard I want it."

"Red, do you want to skip dinner and go straight to dessert?"

She licks her lips, " Sunshine; I'm famished; I must satisfy one hunger before I let you starve me later."

"Good girl."

Just as the words leave my lips, Carrie delivers our food. I can't wait to see which bed this conversation leads to.

III

Red (Asia)

Dinner tasted extra decadent; maybe it was the flirting, or maybe it was just the company.

As we were leaving, Don's Roe called his crew that we would meet up with to cancel on them.

It was a social gathering that we have at least once a week.

He told them to go to Massimo's club and have a good time, and we would meet up again next week.

Roe never cancels on his men. Am I a priority? Nope, he is just confused. We are not in a relationship; this is a fling that will end. We both know that what we have is attraction, not love, but I do feel something for Roe; I just don't know what I feel.

Roe brushes the back of my hand with his thumb, "Red, did you drive here?"

I don't know why, but I smirk, "No, Roe, that's why I wore flats. Kass dropped me off, and I told her I would walk home. Your place or mine, Sunshine?"

He stops rubbing my hand, puts his hand around my waist, and whispers in my ear, "Do you want to be loud or quiet?"

I giggle, "My place it is. I can't break your rule in bed, too."

Roe lives at the compound with most of his men; I have my own place. Massimo helped me find a secure condo in the area. M knows how much my privacy means to me. Nobody knows how to get into my place besides Roe and Massimo. I have a special chip embedded in any crystal jewelry I wear, allowing me access to my house.

Only I know how to calibrate the chip so it works. My condo is more secure than the compound. With just a flick of a switch, it can be soundproof or not. As we rush in the door, I flip the switch. I hope things are about to get delicious.

I turn to Roe, "Pick your poison. Are we going vanilla with toys, or are we going to the playroom?"

As the words roll off my tongue, my shoes fly to the corner where they are housed, and my dress flies over my head.

He smirks, "No time to play, baby; my need for you can't wait."

I reach for his belt, "Good, the paddle is already in my room. Are you ready for dessert?"

"Be my good girl and lead the way so i can spank your sweet cheeks." There's the fire in his eyes that I was looking for! I can't wait for him to ravage me!

Roe

Red leads me to the bedroom. I watch her naked butt sway as we make our way. She knows I prefer her with nothing under her outfits; she is my good girl. I can't wait to redden her ass, she might not think I want to claim her, but she is wrong.

I am ready for a relationship again. I know some of her background. Massimo told me a few things after we rescued her; I will tell Red soon about the danger we found recently because it could be life-changing. But for now, I will give her exactly what she wants: a feast of sexual pleasure.

As we enter her room, I spot the paddle hanging on the wall. Red is posted at the end of her bed, hands on the bed, and legs spread.

She looks at me with burning eyes and says, "Turn this bad girl back into your good girl."

I grasp the paddle tightly, "Don't forget to count, Red, and let me hear that loud, sassy mouth."

"I will never forget when it comes to you, Sunshine. You know how I like it." She retorts as she wiggles her cheeks at me.

I do our regular routine. I caress her ass with five soft circles and then smack it twice with my hand. As soon as she rests her head on the bed, she's ready.

I take a deep breath and then begin. Red likes it hard and fast, she knows she will get ten strikes.

SMACK

"One!" her breath starts to hitch.

SMACK

"Two!"

SMACK

"Three!"

I can smell her arousal, and her juices are pooling.

SMACK

"Four!"

SMACK

"Five!"

With the noises she is making, she is close.

SMACK

"Six! Faster!"

Your wish is my command, Red.

SMACK

SMACK

"Seven! Eight!"

SMACK

SMACK

"Nine! Ten! I WILL BE A GOOD GIRL!"

There we go, and that's what I want to hear!

I flip her and pierce her eyes with mine, "Are you ready for me to satisfy your hunger?"

She unbuttons my shirt, takes it off me, and removes both my pants and underwear. It's a good thing I took my shoes off when we came in.

Red must be starving!

"Ravage me, Sunshine!"

As soon as the words are uttered, I flip her on her back, "Red, let's fill you up."

That was the words she was waiting for; she grabbed my hips and pulled me forward.

"Fill me, take me! I am yours!" She screams, does she mean that?

I won't worry about it right now.

Her wish is my command. I straddle her and slowly slide into her entrance.

"Fast or slow, Red?"

She moans, "Fast and hard! Don't hold back, I want you cumming in me right now! You have me at the edge, baby, and I'm ready to fall. Don't make me wait!"

Yes ma'am!

Why did that turn me on more?

I pound into her as hard and fast as I can; she purrs and soaks the bed with her arousal.

I can feel her muscles tightening, her arms laced behind my neck. I can feel how she is arching her body; she's getting ready to kiss me. That is her favorite way to climax, kissing and moaning into my mouth; it is my favorite, too.

As we climax together, I curl her into my side so we can rest together before I tell her the dreaded dangerous news. I just want to cherish this moment; right now, I feel like a real couple.

I feel like I matter.

We matter.

IV

Red

What time is it?

I feel well-rested; that never happens.

I didn't have a nightmare!

I roll over and stretch, and my arm lands on a naked, godlike chest.

Shit!

He spent the night!

That's my rule: never spend the night!

It's too couply and permanent for me. But I rested, which is very rare for me; the last time I slept all night was when Kass spent the night.

I gaze over his sleeping form.

How could I not notice the sun tattoo on his chest? There is red in the center of the sun, which is odd. But it is a very well-done tattoo.

I just can't figure out its meaning.

Roe looks so peaceful; I could get used to this over time.

We will see how this goes, but these two and half months have given me a small amount of hope.

I slowly move out of bed; I will make him my soft and sweet vanilla protein pancakes. Massimo texted me and asked if I had talked to Roe yet.

I replied, and he told me to hurry up.

I wonder what it could be about.

The pancakes smell so sweet, and they are finally done. I made a fresh pot of caramel coffee just as he likes it. As I pour the coffee into the mugs, Roe comes standing in the doorway in just his boxers.

I smirk, "Hungry for food now, Sunshine? Nice ink, by the way."

He inches toward me, "You like it, Red? I got it because of you, sweet cheeks. You call me sunshine, but I like the rare ones. You know, like the once-every-so-often red sun? But you, do you know why I got the red in the middle?"

I shutter, this is uncharted territory, "Why, Sunshine?"

"I call you Red because you're special to me and one of a kind, so I wanted a piece of you on me. So I figured I'd put you in the sun, which is rare, just like you, so I always have you close to me."

What did he just say? Does Roe have feelings for me? this is definitely uncharted waters, I don't know if I'm ready for this. but why does it make me feel all warm and fuzzy inside? it's like Road knows what I need, before I even know it. Change the subject do something don't stay on this topping of feelings!

"Massimo texted me earlier he said that you had something to tell me? Do you want to tell me before breakfast or after breakfast I don't want the pancakes to get cold?"

He slowly sits down at the table, gets comfortable, and sighs, "After all, I don't want your hard work to go to waste, sweet cheeks."

I just bought my eyelashes and nod; why do I have a sinking feeling in my stomach?

V

Roman

Someone needs to hurry up and marry this woman!

She can cook, she can clean, and she's so beautiful with or without makeup.

It might just be me if she goes along with the plan we have to keep her safe.

I don't know how she's going to react, but I guess I've got to be prepared for everything. She's a very strong, independent woman, and after everything she's been through, maybe she can handle this.

Maybe she's ready to become my wife and stay safe so we can conquer this danger together.

Why do I feel like I'm about to break her heart?

Does she really need to know the danger?

How is she going to react to the plan that we came up with?

As I help her wash the breakfast dishes, I take in the familiar warmth of Red's kitchen. The sunlight pours in through the window, casting a gentle glow over her tidy space. Red has a keen eye for order, and whenever I visit, I do my best to help her maintain that sense of control. It brings her comfort and calms her anxious mind.

Running my fingers softly through her hair, I make sure each strand falls perfectly into place. I lean down and place a tender kiss on her forehead, feeling the warmth of her skin against my lips. Then, I guide her to the couch, urging her to take a seat and relax.

Taking a deep breath, I remind myself that I can do this. There's a flutter of nerves in my stomach, but I tell myself she won't resent me for my intentions. After all, she knows how deeply I care for her, especially since the day I rescued her.

"Red, Massimo wanted me to update you on the trouble we have found. This is going to be a lot of info, so just sit tight, okay?" She nods, so I continue. "Sheila has resurfaced. She has found a contract from when you were first sold. We had her follow up, and we found that she consulted a lawyer. The lawyer determined that the contract is valid. Do you remember signing a contract in 2017?"

Red starts breathing heavy, "Sweet cheeks, calm down. You don't have to answer me just shake your head yes or no; we need to go through this okay? I know this is hard for you but please bear with me I promise we do have a solution."

I see the fear in her eyes; I bet she knows what I'm talking about. I left her chin so her eyes could meet mine, and I mouthed the words, "Breathe in and out."

She finally complies. Her body is starting to relax just with my hand on her chin. Once I know she's in a good place, I continue. I don't like doing this to her, but she needs to know. If anybody can handle this, I know it's her.

"The contract that you signed in 2017 was a contract between you and Vernon Rivers. Rivers is a well-known sex trafficker. You were never in his possession. But we found that Sheila took you to meet him several times. The contract stated when you turned 25, you were to marry him, and when you married him, Sheila would receive $100,000. From the latest Intel that we have, Sheila is searching for you since your 25th birthday is only two weeks away. Sheila wants you back, we found the records where she declared you insane legally but we were able to get those documents to be found false and those documents have been destroyed. But apparently, she is determined to see this contract through. Ever since We rescued you in 2019, Sheila has found other ways to make money. She has been stealing girls left and right and putting them in the different sex rings that she put you in. We were able to access her bank records; she is not broke. She is well off. She has over 2 million dollars in her account, and we did some research, and we found that over half of the money in her bank account has come from Rivers. Baby, breathe."

She starts shifting in her seat. She looks like she's about to break—like a fragile, already broken antique. The hurt in her eyes is apparent.

She is trying to hold back the tears.

She is always strong, but I hate seeing her like this.

"Red, I will do everything in my power to protect you. Massimo and I have come up with a plan. We will not allow Sheila to sell you again. I know you may not like the plan, but don't kill me. I know you can kill me with one strike, so just stay calm and listen, okay?"

She retakes a deep breath and nods.

"Massimo suggested that you marry someone in the Bratva; that way, they can help protect you, and they already know everything that they need to know about you. You would be the safest with one of us. Massimo said we should let you choose who that is. Do you have anyone in mind? He said this needs to look like a real marriage outside the Bratva as well. If you want, we can sit down together and make a list."

She cackles, "You have got to be fucking kidding?! I can't believe Sheila is working with the Devil. I remember Vernon, he looks like he's old enough to be my grandfather; I've done my research on him. He's the most well-known trafficker in all of Chicago. I met him the day after I turned legal, Shelia took me to him, and that's when we signed the contract. All I had to do was initial it since Sheila was technically in charge of me. The only part of the contract that they let me see was about the $100,000. I didn't know it was going to Sheila; I thought I took care of that when I burned down his office where he kept all his legal documents. Apparently, he had backups, so is she really looking for me? She must really want the devil to keep me forever; she's always been material and only cared about money. If I had any other option, I really don't want to get married; when you talked to Massimo, do you think that me marrying someone in our group would really make things easier?"

I sit on the couch beside her and put my arm around her, "Red, that's the easiest solution we can come up with. Our main concern is keeping you safe; we know you can handle yourself, but we want you to have backup, and we don't want you to have to worry about what may happen when Sheila decides how she's going to get you. Apparently she's been working closely with Rivers, the last intel I got from Massimo showed that she's on her way to Chicago. She will be showing her face in our territory in the next couple of days, so we need to get a move on. Does anyone come to mind that you could at least stand to be married to for a short period of time?"

She rests her head in her hands, "Honesty, no! I never found myself worthy of the sanctity that is marriage. I'm not worthy of love, most of the time I don't feel like I'm worthy of being protected. I've created this condo as my fortress so I can lock out the world and only let in those who meet my approval. There are only three people that I trust with my life. One of them is a woman. I trust Kass with all my heart, no matter what I know she would protect me; Massimo is one of the only other people that I trust with my life. I know he can protect me, too, but he is married. I guess that leaves my only option."

She swings her legs onto my lap and puts her lips to my ear, "Well, it's a man. He's my age, he is in Bratva, and he knows me better than anybody else. He's one of two men I allow in my house without permission. He's 6 ft 5 in tall, has one tattoo I know of, and looks like a Greek god. He's the sun to my shine. Roman Hart, will you marry me?"

Did Red flip the script on me?

That's my girl.

VI

Red

That was the hardest thing I have ever done?! I asked Roe to marry me, but he still hasn't answered. I don't know what he's thinking; I can't read his face.

I huff, "So what do you say, Sunshine? Are you going to be tied to me for a while?''

That sounded too sexual, but maybe it will make the thought of being bound to me a little more appealing.

Roe slowly gets up from the couch, "Why me, sweet cheeks? What do I have that our bratva soldiers don't have? Do you think you can handle me full-time, Red?"

Um, excuse me?

Who does he think he is talking to?

Full-time?

This dumb ass thinks he is in control!

I will fix him real quick!

I stand up from the couch, slide my hands around his waist and flip his ass over my shoulder in ten seconds flat!

He's in shock as he crashes onto the couch flat on his back. I spin around before he can react, and I straddle him.

"Sunshine, you are here because I allow you to be." I kiss down his body from his cheek down to his bellybutton. Then kiss up his body to whisper in his ear, "I let you into my fortress, so I trust you and proved I can handle you. So what do you say?"

He yanks my head back, licks my ear, and coos, "I say let's go to the courthouse right now. You are mine, Red. I promise you that will never change. I will die for you. Shelia or the devil will never take you from me."

Why does it feel like my heart just thawed out?

I jumped up, "I will drive. You call the judge. Oh, and you are telling Kass and Massimo this was your idea. Give me ten minutes, and I have the perfect dress."

VII

Roman

How can she manipulate me like that?

Am I mad? No, this was a good kind of manipulation.

I would say yes to anything with her straddled on top of me.

She put my ass on the couch!

I didn't think she could do that!

I pity any man who tries to overpower her.

Red will always be safe with me; no one will take her from me.

I called the judge. He told me we got lucky; his last appointment was canceled. As I hung up the phone, he was preparing the paperwork for us.

I do the only thing that seems right, which is to make a phone call.

She picks up on the second ring, "Brother?"

"Meet me at the courthouse in fifteen minutes, bring your husband. I am getting married."

Before Kass can even gather her thoughts, I hang up the phone.

Hopefully, she will forgive me.

Red

This is it—we are getting married today. I never thought I would be a girl who walks down the aisle, even if it is going to be at a courthouse. I'm not the girl you usually bring home to Mama, and I'm not the girl who wears a ring on her finger. But since this is for my safety and to help end the trafficking ring, I will do it.

I have the perfect dress for today. Kass helped me pick it out when I helped her pick out Roe's birthday outfit. It's a floor-length, red lace corset-type dress with a see-through bodice. I bought this dress thinking I would never get to wear it. Kass said that I should buy it because you never know when fate will try to step in. I didn't really believe that too much, but I wouldn't tell her that.

Kass has the best eye for fashion and has been secretly trying to push Roe and me together for years.

Hopefully, she will accept me, even though this is fake and temporary.

She knows I would never hurt Roe or anyone in our Bratva family.

I just hope I can be half the wife she is.

Roe has always looked up to his sister because she helped guide him when things started going south in the past.

Kass has always had that loving and mothering nature, and I hope she gets her wish of becoming a mother one day.

If I ever get the chance to become a mother, I will never harm my children; they will have a life of luxury and never know the pain I endured. But I don't have to worry about that for a while; my birth control shot is good for another two months.

Roe might not want to take that step with me since this is temporary, but that's okay. However, a very isolated part of me wishes this was a real marriage with Roe, where I have the potential to fall in love with him.

After Renee, I don't know if he will ever love again, but I will make the best of our situation.

As I finally get the zipper zipped, I glance at myself in the mirror. Something is missing. What could it be? My necklace! I should wear my red crystal heart necklace for today; it will pull everything together! I tie my hair up in a half-up, half-down look just to make me look sophisticated.

I don't know why my brain is making a big deal about today, but I might as well enjoy it while I can.

This may be the first and last time I get married.

We will see how this temporary marriage goes, and if it goes well, maybe I'll get married for real one day.

No matter what I know, I will treat Roe how he deserves; he will be cherished like he's never been loved.

When our marriage ends, he will not know who Renee was.

As I take one last look in the mirror, I realize I've come a long way from the girl I used to be.

If you had asked me two years ago if I ever saw myself getting married, I would've told you that marriage is not even on the same planet. But now it's like a hole opened in my heart, just enough to let Roe, that's it.

Even though I know this is fake and temporary, part of me wants to keep him as mine forever. But if he ever asked, I would not tell him that until I'm sure that's how he feels. I've been hurt way too much, just like him.

Okay, I'm ready. I am ready to see what the future holds, ready to see how Roe takes care of me, and prepared to let him see the parts I have been hiding. As I exit my bedroom, I realize that these will be my last moments as Asia Levine, and then I will be Asia Hart.

Why does Asia Hart seem to fit me?

VIII

Roman

The judge just messaged me that everything is ready.

It's time to get temporarily married to Red; Asia will be my wife in a few hours.

Asia Hart....that has a ring to it.

Massimo owed me a favor, so I finally cashed it in.

I sent him a drawing of a custom wedding set. He ordered it for me, but I paid for it. It's not ready today, but it will be here tomorrow; sometimes money is handy.

It's only worthy of Red's finger.

The engagement ring is a 5-carat red diamond heart with a wedding band with black and red alternating diamonds on an infinity band.

Even when this marriage ends, I will let her keep the ring.

She may walk away with more than the ring; Asia deserves the world, and I will give my good girl everything she desires.

"Red, if we are going to get married today, we better leave soon."

Just as I finish the statement, I glance in her room doorway, and there stands the most majestic red angel I have seen!

Her dress is perfect, just like her body. I am glad she chose a red lacy dress; red is Red's color in every sense.

I stroll over to her and slide my arms around her waist, "Red, you look delicious. When we get back, I want to devour you!"

She giggles, "Sunshine, I can't wait to get back to play with you as my husband."

Why does that make me feel warm and fuzzy inside? This woman could become my weakness and I would be okay with it. Part of me wants to give her the life of a princess, I want to make all her hopes and dreams come true.

She is nothing like Renee, Asia is an open book who will tell you everything she wants. Yes Red has a horrible past but most of us in this life have one too. Mine has not been as bad as most because Kass sheltered me from it, but that is why I joined the bratva. We do more good then we do bad, our main goal right now is to end sex trafficking in all of Chicago. Asia has been our greatest source to date of meeting our goal.

"Alright, let's get you married, Red. Then we can see how good or bad you can be."

I feel her shiver with anticipation in my arms. She roughly kisses my lips and leads the way to our future.

IX

Red

As I'm driving to the courthouse, Roe cannot stop staring at me like he wants to eat me.

As soon as we are married, he can eat me anytime.

Asia, get those dirty thoughts out of your head; he's doing this to protect you. For all you know, Roe is going to want to keep this casual but pretend to be married to the outside world.

If I were looking for a man to marry for the long haul, Roe would be it. He is sweet and considerate, and he's always willing to help.

Kass calls him for the littlest things, and he always comes to help.

He knows how to treat a woman and how to respect her.

As I parked and we walked up to the courthouse, I saw two familiar faces standing there.

"I told you that dress would make you look like a goddess!" Kass says as she hugs me and whispers in my ear. "He doesn't know it yet, but you two belong together."

She kisses my cheek and allows Massimo to hug me. Massimo whispers, "Congratulations, be patient with him."

I put on my armored face and replied, "Alright, now that the gang is all here, let's get married!"

Everyone giggles and proceeds inside the courthouse.

Let's do this.

Goodbye Asia Levine, hello Asia Hart!

The name change will definitely take some getting used to.

Roman

Two days later...

Well, that was too easy!

I have officially been married to Asia Hart for two days now.

These few days have been full of craziness; we have only seen each other for eight hours.

I am working with Massimo to track Shelia and the Rivers, which has resulted in me staying back at the compound when I would rather be in bed with my wife.

Massimo gave my wife the week off so Kass and Asia could spend quality time together while we were busy.

Today, they decided to go to the spa. Massimo set them up with a service to get everything done from head to toe. Little does sweet cheeks know, we are going on a little getaway once I get off today.

With Massimo and Kass's help, we are going to Greece for three days.

Massimo and I have been doing extensive research, and it'll be entirely safe for us over there since Rivers and Sheila are here.

I would do anything to make Red happy. While we are on the plane, I will finally give her the custom wedding set. I can't wait to see what Red thinks of the set.

Massimo said it would be a good idea to take just a few days to ourselves, especially to get Red's mind off of everything.

I guess you could call this our mini honeymoon. But I've already compiled a list of things we must do.

Kass gave me a list of things that Red has talked about doing if she ever gets to go to Greece.

The list includes climbing Mount Olympus, going to Balos Beach, and seeing the Parthenon.

Hopefully, we will get to do all three things before we crash back into reality.

A part of me would do anything to make Red smile; she deserves the world.

I must focus on my work with Massimo so I can run off halfway across the world with the woman who makes me shine.

X

Red

I need to start pampering myself more often.

The spa experience was like an out-of-body experience.

My body feels rested, rejuvenated, and like a brand-new person. Plus, my nails look fantastic, with sparkly red French tips.

Kass says she does this at least two times a month. I told her if I could squeeze it in, I'd go with her every time she went.

I'm sure Massimo won't mind since Kass only hangs out with Kiera and me, and we are both a part of the life.

Pampering makes me want to go home, crawl into my bed with a good book, and relax the day away!

A storybook moment occurs as we are about to get in the car with Jared, Kass' driver.

A helmeted man pulls up on the shiniest red Harley I have ever seen!

He is dressed to the nines in a red velvet suit with red velvet boots to match.

This man must be essential or trying to impress a woman. I would definitely be impressed, but I have a thing for bikes and fine-dressed men.

But I shouldn't be looking; I'm a married woman.

But wait—that bracelet he's wearing is a red crystal bracelet with a sun on it!

I made a bracelet like that, but I gave it to Roe.

As the thought leaves my mind, the mysterious biker removes his helmet.

He reveals a fresh, high and tight, and well-groomed sexy beard with a sexy "I will eat you" grin.

Way to make a woman pool between her legs!

"Like what you see, sweet cheeks? Want to hop on?" He smirked like he could own me, but I might just let him.

Is he asking if I want to hop on the bike or him?

Can I have both?

"Can you get me home safe, Sunshine?" I retort as I kiss him on the cheek.

"I can get you to the airport safely. We are not going home. We are going on our honeymoon!" He says as his arms wrap around my waist.

Honeymoon!

He's taking me on a trip?

Is he trying to seduce?

He doesn't have to take me on a trip to do that.

"Oh really? But I don't have anything packed, Roe. A woman can't go anywhere with nothing."

Kass giggles, "That's where I come in! Roe gave me your suitcase earlier, it's in the car. We are following you to the airport. I hope you both have the best time! Don't hate me, Asia, but I gave Roe your bucket list."

She what!

Friends ensure you enjoy life; they love you and want the best for you.

I walk over and hug her, "Thank you, Kass!"

I kiss her cheek as she whispers, "He's falling for you. Prepare yourself and be gentle."

Did he tell Kass how he feels?

Does Roe want to keep me?

Is this marriage real or still fake?

Roe clears his throat. "We don't want to miss the plane. Are you ready to hop on?"

I shake my head and straddle the bike.

As Kass gets in the car, Roe shuts her door and then gets on the bike.

Before we head to the airport, he says, "Don't worry, Red. I have the toys on the plane; we will join the mile-high club."

This man has captured my heart love, here I come.

XI

Roman

3 Days Later...

These three days have been the most memorable and sexual days of my life.

We joined the mile-high club at 35,000 feet.

Red refused for it to be vanilla.

I had brought her favorite toys with us: her spreader bar and a paddle.

Our mile-high encounter started with heavy petting and then turned into Red's legs above her head in the open position, with my face drinking up all her dripping juices.

I will never forget her moaning and purring from that night.

It's like she was mine, to have and to hold. Mine to cherish, mine to never let go.

But that was just the beginning of our honeymoon; all three days were spent finishing her bucket list and trying new positions.

There was never one night or day that we didn't end up in each other's passionate arms.

The best part happened on the plane, and it wasn't the lovemaking.

It was her reaction to her custom wedding ring set.

Never have I ever seen Red cry.

She burst into tears, dropped to her knees, and asked me, "What did I do to deserve this? Where did you find this? I am not worthy of this!"

I explained it all to her like this, "You deserve the world! I designed the ring just for you. It's one of a kind, and it's just like you. This shows you my commitment to you and how my love can grow for you. Yes, Red, I am falling in love with you. I want to make this marriage last and make it real. Nothing will happen to you if you are within my reach."

After that conversation, she confessed that she is starting to feel for me. She didn't say she loves me, but it's definitely a start.

I can see our future; maybe we can have a love like Massimo and Kass one day.

I can see the emotions in her eyes growing; she is growing more affectionate and doesn't shy away from public displays of affection. Massimo mentioned the other day that we look like a real couple.

I sat with Massimo, confessed my feelings for her, and asked for his advice on making it work.

He said, "Love is two-sided and only two-sided. Never let a third side enter the equation. Two is better than one, but three is too many. Always stay open and honest. Treat her like a valuable gift that you don't want to lose. You can see that she's happier, but keep her happy."

I felt like Massimo knew more than he was letting me know, but he didn't want to alarm me.

That's okay; he's the boss, so I trust him.

He has been married for just a little longer than me. Kass and Massimo got married a little over two months ago. They are inseparable, and so is their love. They are a prime example of how love can find a way, even with all the negative in this world.

Since we returned from our quick honeymoon, we have a new sense of each other; we are in sync.

Red knows how I want my morning coffee and how hot to turn the shower.

Yes, these are simple things, but these are significant milestones for newlyweds who went from friends with benefits.

Before, we didn't have to remember anything because I never stayed the night, and we maybe messed around once or twice a month. Now we live together and do everything together. I don't know how I ever used to sleep alone.

Holding someone in your arms to sleep is the best feeling, and it refreshes you when you wake up.

I am already on the road this morning. I hated leaving Red in bed alone, but Massimo texted me late last night to get to the compound early this morning. I grabbed my bike and hit the pavement. I quickly stopped at Don's Diner to get a cup of coffee and pastry since I had to leave Red in bed, but I did text her to let her know where I went.

As I exit Don's, things start to get weird. A figure in a black hoodie is leaning against my bike.

"Excuse me, that's my bike you're leaning on. I need to leave. Can you please move?" I asked the hooded figure.

Instead of turning around, the figure reaches for the hood; instantly, I am on guard because I notice the $10,000 ring on her plastic finger. There's no way this is real! She is supposed to be burnt to a crisp. This better just be a nightmare.

"My Row Row! Aren't you happy to see me, my love?"

Renee Rosenthal, how the heck is she alive?

Why is she hugging me? I'm going to play this off.

"Get your lying hands off me, Renee! Where have you been? Why are you just coming back now? You have been gone for almost two years." I push her off me and sit on my bike.

"Now, Row Row, don't be mad at me! It doesn't matter, babe! I'm back to stay! I have this gorgeous ring that you gave me back. Why don't we get married and start over?" She coos while petting my shoulder.

She's lost her mind if she thinks I would do anything with her lying ass.

Before I can even respond, a beauty in a red jumpsuit is stomping towards us like she's ready to kill.

XII

Red

Who does this silicone bimbo think she is putting her hands on my man?

She must have a death wish!

Wait, no way!

That is Renee!

She is alive, but how?

You know what? It doesn't matter.

I will send her right back to the grave permanently this time.

She just asked my husband to marry her.

She doesn't know me but will know what I allow her to see.

I go full lover mode on Roe; let's see how she reacts. I rush over to Roe, where he's sitting backward on the bike while Barbie has her cold plastic hand on his shoulder.

I pay her no mind, straddle the bike, and stick my tongue down Roe's throat.

I will mark my territory; she doesn't know who she's messing with.

"I missed you, baby. You were supposed to take me with you! You know I can't resist a hot and heavy ride!"

As I finished speaking, Roe caught on to what I was doing, and the realization finally reached his eyes.

"I know, sweetheart. But I didn't want to disturb your sweet dreams. Did you take a taxi here? Well, are you ready to go then? We have a lot to catch up on?" He replies and kisses my pouty face.

"Are you going to introduce me to your pretty friend, baby?" I retort while looking at Renee. Let's see how she plays this.

You can tell her ego gets the best of her as she replies, "Hello darling! I'm Renee Rosenthal, and I'm very shocked to see you kissing my fiancé like that."

She holds up her hand.

I remember what Roe's crew said; she's all about money and material things, but she called that ring cheap. I'm going to play this shit up!

I remove my hands from Roe, hop off the bike, and channel my inner Barbie.

"What!!! Your fiancé? Are you sure?" I grab her hand to look at her ring and then taunt her. "Your ring is so little and cute! You're sure he's your fiancé. I'm so sorry, but that's impossible!"

I let the fake tears flow, which I have perfected over the years.

I sneakily reach into my pocket and hit my SOS button; Massimo will be on his way in about two minutes.

She looks at me with sad but curious eyes, "Why is it impossible, darling? Row Row and I have been together for a long time."

The audacity of this woman knows no bounds.

Does she really think I am that dumb?

Okay, it's time to play with her some more.

"Well, answer me this, Renee, you see my ring?" Her eyes dart to my hand and land on my five-carat custom wedding set. "What do you think of it? Isn't it just so darling?"

She is taking in my ring and my stance, I hope she can see where I'm going with this.

She replies, "Darling, that flashy thing would never come from a man with class. The man that gave that to you must have done something so wrong that he figured a big present would make up for it. He probably cheated on you and didn't want you to find out. Tell her Row Row big gifts don't mean more. It's the gifts that come from the heart."

I let out a haunted laugh, "Funny you should say that to Row Row." I take the black and red crystal men's wedding band out of my back pocket and slip it on my sunshine's finger. "Baby, you left this on the nightstand." I hadn't given it to him because I had helped make it for him with Massimo's elite jeweler.

Renee looks pissed, but she is pissed at the perfect time because I see Hailey in place.

She will take the shot when I give the signal.

"What the fuck do you think you're doing, little bitch? Roman belongs to me. You and him must have been playing house while I was gone! But that shit ends now!"

"Yes, it does because you can't have him. He's my husband, and you're dead."

I snap my fingers, and the silent shot races through the air.

It reaches the target in seconds, dead center of Renee's skull. She is not returning from the dead this time; Hailey doesn't miss.

Roe lets the crew in Don's know since no tourists are here this early, and we begin the clean-up outside.

It only takes us ten minutes tops to clean up the entire scene and make it look like nothing happened here.

No one will ever know who died here today because, as far as the world knows, she died years ago.

Well, she is definitely dead this time.

Let's see how Roman handles this.

This could be the end of our relationship or the push we needed.

XIII

Roman

The cleanup is complete, and we all convene at Massimo's place.

"What the fuck happened?! Can someone please explain to me why a dead woman just died again? I felt like I was living a nightmare all over again!" All my emotions just start flowing out of me. I feel like I am either broken or all my emotions finally have broke the surface of my stoney heart.

"Relax, Roman." Massimo pats my shoulder, "Just sit back and listen so I can explain." I take a deep breath and nod. "We found out Renee was alive as soon as you returned from your honeymoon. Turns out she followed you to Greece, but somehow missed that y'all are married. She's never been the brightest woman, but she appears to have been watching you since my wedding. But that's not the part that scared us. Asia only knows that she was watching you for awhile she doesn't know the rest. Renee gave Shelia and Rivers her location before she died. We found the device on her when we were removing her body. So now they may be moving soon, so we need to be on the lookout. I know Asia is shaken up about today, but she was a real professional. I am very proud of how safe and controlled she kept the situation. She possibly saved your life. We think Renee wanted revenge for her husband's death. We found out how she survived. There was a mole in our Bratva; he has been dealt with and will spend eternity with Renee. We must protect our women more than ever now, and we can't lose what holds us together."

I nod, "Yes, boss. I understand. I will do anything in my power to protect our women."

My phone buzzes in my pocket, but I ignore it.

Massimo pats my shoulder again, "How does it feel to be in love with your wife?"

I sigh, "It is a foreign feeling, but it feels right. She couldn't be more perfect; she is the complete opposite of Renee. She's my angel."

Massimo laughs, "Welcome to the club! You want a drink?"

I just nod. Before he even hands me a drink, all hell breaks loose.

Shots fly through the compound for five minutes straight. Glass shatters everywhere, and three men lose their lives.

I hear Massimo screaming after we are sure the shooters are gone, "Kass, where are you? Kass?!"

Oh shit! I forgot the women were here with us. Just in time, I rush to Massimo's side to see Kass rush towards us and hug us both.

I gather my thoughts, "Kass, are you okay? What happened?"

I hug her again, I'm so glad my sister is safe. She has found her place in this Bratva world.

She takes a deep breath, "We killed six of the shooters, but I hate to say it, Code Red."

What the hell! I feel my chest start to constrict.

Before I can ask, Massimo replies, "Who did they take and who took them?"

She looks at me with those sad eyes and replies, "After we killed what we thought was the last shooter, Shelia had breached the compound, and she took Asia with her. She shot a needle in Asia's upper thigh, which caused Asia to collapse. I was on the other side of the compound when I saw it, and I'm sorry I couldn't reach her in time before Shelia and Rivers ran out with her."

There goes my world! They took my wife!

I'm not fading into the abyss, and I will not lose my balance.

It's time to get my wife back.

I looked at Massimo. "Let's get to work. I just promised I wasn't going to lose her. I will not break that promise! Boss, did you put the tracker in her ring like I asked?"

Massimo smiles, "Yes, remember we protect our women."

I smirk, "They better hope I get the pleasure of killing them because if I don't, I fear Asia may make them suffer."

Massimo puts his arm around Kass. " That's true, especially Shelia. Asia has always said that if given the chance, she would get revenge."

Kass looks at Massimo with love and regret, "Confession time. Asia swore me to secrecy! She figured they would strike soon, and she had a plan; revenge was putting it lightly. She is aiming for their lives. Oh, and I almost forgot! When you get her location I need to alert the others in on her plan so we can get all the other girls out. Asia discovered Rivers was bringing his entire ring with him, so we have to rescue eighty girls. Just in case Asia gave me all eighty-five moonstone rings she made for the girls, she said it helps build them back up and give them a new start."

Kass pulls the bag of rings out of her purse. Why is my wife always caring more for others than herself? Why did she come up with this plan without me? Doesn't she know I would do anything and everything for her?

Kass sees my wheels turning, "She didn't want to include you or Massimo because she knew you both would do everything in your power to stop her. She would do anything to keep you both safe because she knows how hard you both work to save everyone else. She wants to do this for herself and prove to both of you that she no longer needs rescuing! She just wants to be equally viewed as a member of the Bratva and equally as a partner. She loves you both and just wants you to realize. Massimo, she looks at you like her other big brother. Roman, she has admitted to me how much she loves you. She needs to do this to heal properly, so let's help her and let her, okay?"

Well damn, Red has confided in my sister. Red is serious about us and our marriage. Red might love me, but as soon as this is over, I will tell her how much she means to me, and I swear it!

"Fine, Kass, how long do we have to wait until we can go get her? We will let her do this her way, but only within reason." Massimo says, still while holding and comforting Kass.

I long to hold my sweet cheeks already; this will be tough.

Kass sighs with relief: "I am so glad you agreed. We have to wait one month before we go get her. Trust me, there is no way this can fail. We have a foolproof plan. They will both be dead in one month. Asia is wearing a different crystal necklace right now. Her everyday necklace is to get in her house, but we switched it out for the crystal necklace she had the jeweler make when she made your ring, Roe. This necklace has a trigger on the clasp to open the crystal to drip poison out of it, and it only takes three drops of this particular poison to kill the average male. The amazing part is Asia is immune to this poison because she has been slowly introducing this poison into her diet as a precaution. Asia has been plotting her revenge for years, but I have just started to help carry it out recently. She has this under control, guys; we just have to trust our girl."

An entire month am I leaving my wife in the hands of the devil and she-devil? Are these women insane?

I take a deep and calming breath, "Fine, but they better not leave a single mark on her! I know her body from head to toe. If she even has one hair out of place, I will end whoever touched her!"

Kass chuckles, "We get it, brother! You love her, and nobody harms what is yours. Here, Roe, she left her rings and left you a note."

Kass puts both in my hand as she and Massimo exit the room.

Let's see what my Red says; she even wrote it in red ink.

It reads:

Sunshine,

I f Kass gives you this letter, just know everything is going according to plan. I will protect you, Massimo, and the Bratva with all my being! I need to do this; I need closure. Shelia and Rivers have been *haunting me since I was young. I will no longer let them haunt my dreams; I want my dreams to be filled only with us and our love. I love you, Sunshine. Yes, this is the first time I have said the words to you, but I promise that when this is over, I will look you in your beautiful eyes and tell you as you hold me in your arms. Stay strong, my love. I will see you soon. LOVE, Your RED <3*

I hear you loud and clear, my love. I will see you in thirty days, not a day later.

XIV

Red

29 Days later....

I never expected revenge to be this tiring. Sheila and Rivers have been working me to the bone since they brought me here.

But everything has been falling into place. They are both almost fully poisoned, and they will get the last dose at the ceremony tomorrow.

These idiots still don't know that Roe and I already got married. I have been tasked with planning Vernon and my wedding. I am making it scarce and very dull. Why would I do that, though? Because it's not a wedding—it's their funeral.

They have haunted me for years, and Sheila has tortured me since the day she took me in. She is lucky I didn't have her murdered before now; she is responsible for the darkest part of my life. She is the reason I find it so hard to love.

I am sure Massimo has read my file, but I don't know if Roe knows. After we signed the contract with Vernon, Sheila decided it was a good idea to sell my virginity.

She sold my virginity for $50,000. I didn't have a choice. I was not ready for that; it broke me.

The man that raped me, I never saw his face, but I will never forget his scent or his voice.

He wore a mask the entire time. His voice was very raspy, and he smelled of sandalwood.

He only told me to call him Dust because, after that night, I would never see him again unless he saw fit.

I have not come face to face with him since that degrading night. But if I do find him or he finds me, he better be prepared to suffer; I never forget a criminal, especially a criminal that made me want to end my life.

How he spoke to me and touched me made me realize that he had to be a criminal. I tried to end my life by taking half a bottle of Sheila's sleeping pills and downing half a bottle of whiskey with them. That was the only time she saved my life and the only time she took me to the hospital.

After she brought me back home, I remember her exact words, "You are not allowed to die until I say so! You are my source of income, and I'll be damned if I ever give that up!"

That's all I have ever been to anyone is a source of income or a body to warm their bed. Until I met Roe, he respected me and made me feel loved. Never in my nightmares does life turn into a fairy tale, but my reality has, and I wouldn't change it for the world.

If my plan succeeds, that will be the last sex tracking ring in Chicago, and our city will be free.

I have been lucky this month because Vernon wants me to have "a virginal essence" until our dreaded wedding night. This is good for me because my body has felt off since we returned from the honeymoon. I have felt sluggish and always hungry for a few days here.

Usually, I can go for days or weeks without feeling hungry or tired, so this is a new feeling for me.

But once this mission is over, I'll take care of myself.

My main focus is ending this sex ring, and taking down as many criminals as possible. Everything else will have to wait.

I am on my way to meet Vernon, he says he has someone he wants me to meet before the "wedding" tomorrow. Anyone Vernon wants me to meet is probably just as low as him. Let's just get this over with so everything flows into place.

I know on the reception hall door. I hear Vernon shout, "Enter!"

As I enter, I see a figure standing next to Vernon, and the figure has his back to me. From the back, he looks well kept. I recognize the suit from a designer commercial. As I approach them, my body starts to tense, and the smell of sandalwood reaches my nose. This can't be happening to me right now! Calm down, Asia. Let's just see how this goes.

Veron begins to speak, "Sweetheart, you made it! I would finally like you to meet my oldest friend, Vito Vincent. He will be officiating our ceremony tomorrow."

Vincent speaks with a raspy growl, "Hello, darling. We finally meet again."

What the fuck! It's him! It's Dust, the asshole that raped me! But Vito Vincent, I know that name. Oh shit!! That's

Renee's husband. How the fuck is he alive too? I can't breathe!

Vernon looks at Vito, "What do you mean?"

Dust smirks, "Remember when I told you I bought a virgin and I came back with a bloody neck from her fighting me and trying to get me to stop? Meet the culprit of that scratch."

Vernon looks at me and laughs, "Well damn, all the fight has left her body as she grew up. She's been a very docile woman." He sauntered over to me and put his arm around my waist, "This marriage will allow us to expand our trafficking ring. I have big plans like ending the Ballentine Bratva."

I don't react; they are looking for a reaction.

Vito replies, "I can't wait to get Roman so I can torture him and find out what he did to my wife."

Vernon spins me and presses his old cracked lips to mine; I am trying to hold back the throw-up.

"We will get revenge for her, Vito, I promise." Just as he finishes his sentence, he starts coughing up blood. The poison is beginning to get to his organs.

I pat his back, "Are you alright? Do I need to go get your water or medicine?" I play the concerned lover when really I wish his death came now.

If only I hadn't given the crew a 30-day time frame, I would be ready to end this now! Especially since I now know Vito is alive.

The mole must have saved them both, not just Renee.

Vernon replies, "No, I'm fine. But get us the good whiskey. We have much to discuss and celebrate! After that, sweetheart, you can go finish your wedding preparations. Remember, sweetheart, I want you to be clean-shaven and ready for me."

Don't react like you normally would. Channel the dutiful lover. "Yes, sir, I understand," I reply and excuse myself. I walk out with my eyes glued to the floor. As soon as I'm in the hall, I'm back to myself.

I make my way to the room where they keep the alcohol. I grab a bottle of the most expensive stuff and two glasses. I know they are going to finish this bottle tonight, so it's a good thing this bottle was already opened.

Since the seal on the bottle is already broken and some of the whiskey is missing, I will make up for it. I slip the rest of the poison into the whiskey. This amount of poison could be the final blow to Vernon, but it will only make Dust sick to the point of weakness.

I walk back to the reception hall knock and bring them their alcohol. I can't stand these two idiots.

Vernon coughs, blood landing on his handkerchief. "Thank you. Run along and prepare for tomorrow. Tomorrow is a day of happiness and reckoning!"

Both Vernon and Vito laugh as I graciously take my leave. Their death will bring me an abundance of joy.

Over the last few weeks, the halls have become increasingly desolate, and Vernon hasn't noticed yet. I have been able to slowly start sneaking women to safety. There were eighty women here when I arrived, but now the numbers are dwindling.

So far, I have been able to get twenty women out.

I gave them a crystal necklace and told them where they could meet a member of the Ballentine Bratva.

That puts our total at sixty women we need to save tomorrow. I am ready for this mission to be over.

Before I head to my room, I check on Sasha, whom I have grown close with. Vernon took her the day after I got here.

We have conversed a lot, and I found that this was her first time in the ring, and she was not ready for it. I helped her after her first encounter, and we have bonded ever since.

As I knock on her door, I hear her sobbing. I enter without thinking, "Sasha, are you okay? What can I do?"

She is sitting on the floor, crossed-legged in tears, with her hands bound. "I'm so sorry, Asia, they forced it out of me. You know I would never intentionally betray you! They said they know you. I swear they didn't hurt me; they just threatened me and tied me up!"

I reach her level and untie her, "Calm down, Sasha. Everything will be okay if you're not hurt; that's what matters. Who was it?"

Before Sasha answered, I heard a whisper coming from my left side.

A whisper that I have longed to hear, a whisper that makes me pool.

"Hello, Red. Did you miss me?"

It takes me a few seconds to comprehend that this is real and not a fairy-tale.

Only one person in the entire universe calls me Red, and only one person ever will.

XV

Roman

Red looked at me with a rejuvenated fire; I barely had time to stand my ground before she leaped into my arms and wrapped her luscious legs around my waist.

She doesn't hesitate to slip her arms around my neck and shove her magical tongue down my throat.

As I come up for air, "Sunshine, you're early!" She maintains a whisper and hops down, "What is the plan? What are you doing?"

Before he can answer, Sasha whispers, "Well this is awkward. How do you know each other?"

Red giggles, "Sasha, I'm sorry I got excited. This is Roman Hart, my husband."

Sasha begins to panic, "Husband? Hart? The one they are waiting for? The one Vernon wants dead? Oh shit! I'm screwed. They are going to kill me!"

My wife can handle anything.

She walks over to Sasha and rubs her back.

"Breathe. Everything will be fine. I already have a plan in place. I'm sure Roe brought backup, and we can get you out now. Let's get you to safety, and then I will explain all this when it's over, okay?"

Sasha nods. I hit the button, and Hailey enters.

Hailey hugs Asia then leads Sasha to safety.

Red turns to me, "What's the plan?"

I smirk, "You're going to cut me up and bruise me, then play dutiful lover and take me to Vernon."

She smiles, "Baby, I'll rough you up any day. But be aware, Vito is with Vernon. He's alive, and I recently learned he's the man that raped me when I was younger."

It is taking everything in my power to night go on a murdering spree! Not only is he alive, but he raped Red!

I put my arms around her and kissed her cheek, "Beat me before I go murder every criminal I find!"

"Only because you asked nicely. But you have to beat me later, deal?" She smirks.

"Deal!"

She kisses me one last time, don't fuck with my wife.

She is scary.

She slaps like a professional; I'm holding back tears! Damn that stings. Then she takes my knife and cuts open my shirt; she kisses my chest and then slides the blade across my skin. She only went deep enough to make me bleed.

I hand Red the blood-red rope, and she ties my wrists.

This is hot, so we will do this again when we get home.

"Take me to them, the crews in place."

XVI

Red

This man never ceases to amaze me!

I can't believe he showed up days earlier than planned, but I can't blame him. He doesn't want to see me even fake married to anyone else.

I led him to the reception hall and barged in.

As I enter, I hear, "What the fuck is going on?"

Of course, it's Vernon, I snap into character.

"Look what I found trying to steal some of the women! Vernie, how did he find us? He's going to ruin the ceremony!"

Vernon smirks; he's getting aroused. His nostrils are flaring, and his pants are getting tight, not that his pants need to be any tighter when they're holding his pregnant looking belly in.

"Sweetheart, we will take care of him; nothing will ruin our big day!"

He can barely get the words out.

He's slurring so severely.

Vito is next to form part of a sentence, "Kill him! Death, vengeance, Renee!"

They have only been drinking for about an hour, but the whiskey bottle is empty.

But one of the best parts of the poison is when you mix it with alcohol; you kill your body faster.

It's a good thing nobody but me knows that fact.

"Sweetheart, come kiss me."

Great.

Now, I have to try not to throw up.

This grandpa doesn't do anything for me.

Now's the perfect time to pretend to kiss and stab him! If I take him out, I can torture Dust; that's what I will do. Revenge is mine, mine alone.

I will use my hair as a shield so Vito won't see me pull the knife from between my twin D cups. I lean into Vernon and whisper in his ear as I pull out my knife, "You will never haunt anyone again." I slice his neck from ear to ear, stab him in the heart, and let his body drop to the ground.

As I turned my attention to Vito, I noticed Sunshine already had him tied up.

Roe chuckles, "Ready to play with him, Red?"

I kiss him while my chest is covered in Vernon's blood and reply, "Always, revenge will be Red!"

Roman

This woman is scary and sexy, all wrapped into one! It's like nothing fazes her.

She just killed Vernon in ten seconds and is ready to torture the man who raped her. She may be damaged and deranged, but she's only like that because she can't stand criminals who abuse women and take away their rights.

Most women would be grossed out by the blood and the dead body, not Red.

She comes alive because she knows how many women she's protecting.

I am not grossed out by her body pressed against me while covered in blood, I find it arousing.

She is the boss; she directs me, "Sun, go in the closet directly behind me. You will have Vernon's bag, what he used to call his okay bag."

I smile and say, "Yes, dear."

She gets Vito situated on the cold metal chair in the middle of the empty reception hall.

He spits, "You dumb girl! You think you can kill me? Vernon was weak; I am not weak, but I will fight! Plus, you will never find my crew."

Red doesn't have to say anything; I answer as I walk over with the bag, "Your crew of thirty men is dead, and your compound is burnt to the ground. We found the address in Renee's phone."

He goes pale and has nothing else to say, so I open the bag and gasp, "Baby, are you going to use all of this on him?"

The bag is full of random things, but random things that can either hurt, kill, or pleasure.

The contents of the bag include pliers, kitchen knives, dildos, rope, lube, and butt plugs.

What was Vernon into?

Red answers," I don't know yet; love depends on what you want to see! You want him to suffer or have pleasure, or both?"

She's a sneaky little woman.

I reply, " How about we torture him and make him watch us please each other?"

Arousal immediately enters her eyes: "What Sunshine wants, Sunshine gets!"

She kisses me sloppily but passionately.

I look at her lovingly, "Let the revenge be fun and messy!"

She laughs cynically, "It's always fun with you!"

Vito's face becomes green; the next thing I know, he is vomiting all over the floor.

"Please, show remorse! Don't harm me; I will do anything you ask!"

She tisks, "Oh, you poor thing! It's way too late for that. I am out for blood and revenge! We have killed Shelia, so you're the last chore to be marked off my list. You will suffer, you will die, and I will never feel regret for removing your existence for this world."

Well, hot damn! That speech got me excited.

She's right. We killed Shelia as soon as we arrived; she's the whole reason Red's in this situation. But I know she is trying to rile him up.

"Please, no! Please let me join the Ballentine Bratva! I can change it. Please, you're a woman. Have mercy!" At this point, Vito has pissed himself and is in tears.

Let's see how Red takes this.

Damn, he must have triggered her!

Red cackled, "You're the dumbest criminal I have ever met! If you did any research at all you would know how dangerous I really I am! I am the head spy for the Balletine Bratva! I have the second-highest kill number in the entire Bratva! Oh, and your best dead friend didn't know I had been poisoning him all month long! Because you drank the whiskey, you are poisoned too, so rather I kill you now or let the poison do it really doesn't matter! I am who I am because you and Shelia treated me like a piece of property, and they could use it anytime they wanted! Well, that comes to an end right now, Dust! Mercy is not in my vocabulary when it comes to criminals who harm women and abuse them! Vernon's bag is going to be the key to your pain. So you will suffer at my hand, and today is your death day!"

She turns to me, still strong and powerful, but there is a hint of regret. "I am sorry you had to hear and see me like that, my love. But dumb criminals and woman abusers are my biggest pet peeve, and he underestimated me, which is a big mistake. Do you want to help me end him, or do you just want to watch? I know how fun watching can be."

Well, she's got me there, "What kind of husband would I be if I didn't help? You boss me, baby, and I'll do everything you tell me to."

She kisses me roughly, "Let's make him suffer so we can play!"

Play? Is she getting bothered by this? Damn, my girl has some kinks!

Your wish is my command, Red.

XVII

Red

The poor criminal, it was clear he was not prepared to die yesterday.

But he did.

He died after four and a half hours of torture.

We did things I have done to people and others that I haven't.

Roman helped me torture Vito until he bled out.

My favorite part was removing each fingernail one by one with just a pair of pliers. Vito screamed, cried, and crapped himself. Before I deliver the most degrading blow, I let Sunshine have some fun.

After removing his fingernails, Sunshine used a kitchen knife to slice off each finger one by one slowly.

The final blow, if I didn't kill Vito by stabbing him in the chest and slicing him open from chest to pelvis, he would have died from embarrassment. Because sliced off his penis right at the base. He didn't deserve to have one since he used it for rape and abuse.

Never will a woman have to fear being kidnapped and sold in the sex ring. Chicago is officially free from sex trafficking.

We burned Vernon's compound to the ground and made sure that there were no criminal survivors. We got all the women to safety, and all the criminals perished painfully in the fire.

No more sex trafficking may mean I can relax for a while. Maybe I can take time to see what's happening with my body.

I am supposed to meet with Kass next week to start our new spa routine, and apparently, she has some big news to tell me.

After this crazy and depressing month, girl time can make everything better.

I know it's only been one day, but Roman seems to be shying away from me. He hasn't wanted to be intimate since we arrived home.

Did I scare him with the torture? Does my body repulse him?

He slept with me last night, but that is all we did. We didn't have sex, and he would not cuddle me.

Could he be concerned if Vernon touched me? I am sure he knows I would never let that happen.

Hopefully, this is just a rough patch we are going through, and things will quickly go back to normal.

My stomach is in knots, and I feel like I could throw up at any second.

There it goes. I just lost all the contents of my stomach. I normally have a strong stomach, so I need help. I need this fixed.

Now!

XVIII

Roman

Having her back is a gift, but I don't know what happened last month.

Did Red have sex with Vernon or any other man in the ring?

She has had to sleep with them once or twice from her past missions, so her cover isn't blown.

But now, if she did sleep with them, that was her cheating on me and her showing she doesn't want to stay in this marriage. Does she want our marriage to continue since she is safe now?

Or does she want to be rid of a husband?

Do I want to stay married to her?

Should I just let her go?

Should I have Massimo reassign me so I don't have to see her?

My heart and brain are all fuzzy.

Which should I follow, my heart or my brain?

Part Two

XIX

Red

It has been an entire week that I have been home.

I love the freedom I have! I don't have to get violent or workout everyday.

But I am still very nauseous throughout the day. Hopefully, I will get that figured out soon. I just want to feel like myself again.

I am meeting up with Kass today, I am still curious what her big news is.

Today I feel like I need to be pampered, especially after all the shit I am dealing with from Roman.

He won't even kiss me! If I try to kiss him, he will only give me his cheeks! I still cook him breakfast, but he doesn't eat it.

He will drink the coffee I make him, but he will just push the food around the plate.

I bet he thinks I am trying to poison him, but I would never do that to the person I love.

Sunshine has become my world, but it feels like he's trying to push me out of his world.

Does he still love me?

Or was I really just a fling?

Is our marriage over?

I need to relax.

It's time to go meet Kass.

XX

Kass

I am a nervous wreck as I wait for Asia at the spa.

My news is significant, and I have only told M and Key.

They are both excited, but Key is mad that she and Marcus are away for the next year.

M, on the other hand, was not thrilled when I told him he went into worry mode.

I need this girl's time, and I feel like Asia might be happy for me.

Here she comes; let's see how today goes.

Here comes Asia. As she sees me, it looks like a weight has been lifted off her shoulders.

That's good; she really needs to relax today.

With the big news, I have something important to ask her.

"Hey, honey! Ready to relax and unwind?"

She smiles, "Of course Kass! Your brother has been a real pain in my ass lately, so I would rather be hanging with you. Besides, you're so much sweeter than him!"

I hug her, I know Roe has been struggling since Asia got back, but we will get to the bottom of it today.

"Come on, Asia. Let's go get started with our massage, and let's let all our tensions fall into someone else's hands."

She hugs me tightly, "Okay, no more negative thoughts, only positive! Let's go!"

After our two-hour massage, I feel like a rejuvenated woman!

Kass is carrying herself with more confidence, and she looks less tense.

Now it's time for our pedicures, which will give us a chance to talk. I will be able to tell her my tiny secret.

We picked our toe colors, and of course, we both chose red. I chose a bright stop sign red, and Asia chose a maroon red. We know what color our men like, but I doubt that is why Asia picked it this time.

Breathe in, Breathe out, Kass! Everything will work out. Remember what Dr Sara said: you must regulate your breathing and emotions.

Okay, I can do this, "Asia, I have a little gift for you. It's a surprise that I will tell you my news!"

XXI

Red

K ass is ready to tell me her news!

"Hit me with it, Kass! But you didn't have to get me a gift."

She smiles and hands me a little red box. "Open it! There's no commitment, I promise!"

That was a weird comment.

I lift the lid of the box, and there's a note in red ink that reads:

> *"I know you're my aunt, but you be my godmother as well?"*

Umm, what does that even mean mean? I lift the paper and see a onesie that says, "Baby Ballentine, coming soon."

What?! Kass is pregnant? Am I going to be an aunt? Kass and Massimo trust me enough to take care of their baby?

I feel the tears forming, and I can't hold the dam back.

I cry, "Of course I will! I can't believe you both trust me that much!"

I can't control the tears; I shake as well.

Kass puts her arm around, "There's another surprise. Kiera is the other godmother. We decided to have two godmothers instead of a godfather and godmother. That's because we know no matter what, Roe will not be able to stop spoiling the baby."

Here goes a more giant dam, "Awe, Kass! How did the boss react? That's why you're not getting your fingernails done like usual!"

I have been hanging on to Kass for dear life, and my emotions are all over the place.

Kass just giggles, "Bossman, went into Papa Bear mode! I am not allowed to lift anything or walk more than six feet without him breathing down my neck! But in his defense, after we talked to Doctor Sarah, I am considered a high-risk pregnancy. Just because I have cerebral palsy and an irregular heartbeat, they are worried that I won't be able to deliver the baby naturally, meaning they are concerned that my body will not be strong enough to push this munchkin out. But I will do everything I can to bring this little one into this world, even if it means it is my time to go."

What the hell?

The doctor is concerned for Kass? That's why she is making sure the baby is taken care of!

She knows that there is the possibility that she could die!

She seems okay with that, but why?

"Kass! That's a big deal! We must do everything we can to ensure you're healthy and have an easy pregnancy! We need you! All of us do, especially Roe and Massimo! I will do everything I can to help through this. That way all your worries are addressed. Also, no stress is allowed! You are not allowed to have another seizure. We will wrap you in bubble wrap if we have to!"

My anxiety is now at an all-time high!

I will protect Kass with my life, and nothing will happen to her or the munchkin.

As I gather my stuff and my emotions, we check out and get in Jared's car.

"Asia, don't treat me like I am broken. I am pregnant, not handicapped!" She laughs, "Okay, well I am both, but you get my point! I will still go to the gym to train, and I will still train the girls. I have already cleared it with Bossman and Doctor Sarah. So know buts! I know how your mind works!"

I pout, "Fine!" I roll my eyes and continue, "But I will be there every step of the way! Tell Massimo to get ready to be sick of me! I will be at all of the appointments."

Kass just laughs and hugs me, "Yes, mother."

Is Karma prepping me for the rest of what she has planned?

XXII

Kass

As we are driving to my apartment, Asia starts to look funny.

"Honey, are you alright?"

She can't hear me; she's clutching the gift box for dear life. I touch her forehead, no fever, but she is sweating profusely.

"Asia, are you okay? Tell me what's wrong?"

Next thing I know, she has her head out the open window and is vomiting profusely for two and a half minutes straight before she sits back in the seat.

She looks at me wide-eyed, "I think I need a doctor. Kass, I've been throwing up since before the kidnapping, and I haven't been myself since then."

Before the kidnapping? So, over a month ago?

Asia is on the birth control shot, but she skipped her last appointment because of the kidnapping!

"Asia, I'm calling Doctor Sarah! She will meet us at my place. Honey, I know this is a lot, but you might be pregnant."

She looked at me with fear and replied, " If he doesn't love me anymore, how will he love his baby?"

She lays her head on me and cries until she falls asleep.

I don't want her to ever feel like this. Does she think Roe doesn't love her anymore? I have to find out what is really going on between them. If she really is pregnant, things are about to get even tougher for her and Roe, I fear.

But let's not get ahead of ourselves. Let's see what the doctor has to say.

When we arrive at Massimo and my apartment, Jared carefully carries Asia inside. M and Roe are out on a drug mission, so they will not be home until late tonight or tomorrow.

I looked at Jared. "Go do anything else Massimo instructed you; do not tell him anything about what's happening! Or so help me; I will make you suffer! This stays between us until Asia has a choice!"

Jared looks at me and bows his head, "Yes, my queen."

XXIII

Red

I still pretended to be asleep as Kass was scolding Jared. I know how scary Kass can be. I do not want to be the object of her wrath.

I stretch and make a show of waking up.

Kass laughs, "I know you were pretending to be asleep; I know how scary I am to other people, but you don't need to worry about that. My wrath will never be directed at you. I just wanted you to find out what's happening and decide before the whole Bratva family knows."

She's such a mama bear, "Thank you. Kass, I am terrified! If I am pregnant, I fear that's not going to bring your brother back to me. He's been shying away from me; he doesn't want to be intimate with me, and he will not eat my food. I don't blame him for the food part because he knows a poisoned

Vernon and Vito, but being intimate? I have no idea what's stopping him there. This mission was done differently this time. Sorry for all the intimate details. On most missions, I had to sleep with some of the men to keep my cover secure, but I got lucky this time. Vernon claimed he wanted our wedding night to be perfect and virtuous, so we never had intercourse. Vernon wouldn't allow any of his men to touch me either. Honestly, I would have fought for my life and marriage because I would never cheat on Roe. I am fully committed to him and only him. But I don't know where he stands."

She looks at me with sadness and concern, "We will figure him out, don't worry. It's not too intimate, but I know there are some things you don't want to tell me about because I'm Roe's sister, and I respect that. But you went above and beyond to protect the city and your marriage! Does Roe know that? I'm sure his tune would change if he knew the lengths you went to! I can't stand how stubborn men can be."

She hugs me and rubs my head as a knock sounds on the door. Doctor Sarah has arrived.

I sit up straight and gather my emotions; let's figure this out so my life can get back to normal.

Doctor Sara asked me a series of questions and I answered truthfully.

She replies, "Okay, take this pregnancy test and go take it in the bathroom. We should know in about five minutes if you are pregnant. To me, it sounds very likely."

Breathe, Asia. Breathe. It's not the end of the world if you're pregnant. It could be a new beginning for you, and you could give the child a life like you never had.

I nod in the doctor and Kass's direction and head to the bathroom.

These are going to be the longest five minutes of my life.

I pee on the stupid stick; why is a test giving me so much anxiety? I wash my hands and sit on the toilet.

I will not leave this room until I know what the future holds.

XXIV

Kass

As Asia exits the bathroom, the answer is written all over her face.

I stride to her and hold her as she collapses in my arms. The tears won't stop falling; we are both a crying hormonal mess.

I hand the test to Doctor Sara and try to dry up my tears. I rub Asia back. Together, we will get through this.

Doctor Sara says, "Okay, it's confirmed you're pregnant. I brought my portable ultrasound machine. Would it be okay if I did a trans-vaginal ultrasound to see how far along you really are? It doesn't hurt. It is a pinch and some cold liquid."

Asia nods, "As long as Kass is right here with me."

I kissed her forehead to calm her. "Like you said, Asia, you will get annoyed with me because I'm not going anywhere."

That was the right thing to say.

Asia smiled, and her tears were gone in an instant.

XXV

S

What in the actual fuck is wrong with these women?!

They spend the whole day at the spa, then have a private doctor's appointment at their house!

How spoiled can they be?

They have good, hardworking men.

What are they doing? They are galloping around town and spending money however they please; somebody must stop it!

If I had Massimo and Roman, they would never be taken advantage of. Plus, I wouldn't need their money.

All they would have to do is want and love me.

I know I have my kinks, but it is nothing I can't handle.

I would treat those men like the kings they are, not the ATM these women treat them as.

No worries, give it a few months, and I will take care of Asia and Kassani once and for all.

Then Roe and Massimo will be mine!

XXVI

Red

The transvaginal ultrasound made me uncomfortable, and I have done some crazy things!

It was overwhelming, and it made me feel like I needed to poop.

Kass and I are exactly the same amount into our pregnancy, six weeks.

Kass says she'll be there for me every step of the way, and I will do the same for her.

We have our first appointment together in two weeks; I am scared but excited.

I will give this baby the best life possible!

Kass texted Massimo he and Roe will be home in just a few minutes.

Jared brought me back to my place so I could get settled and prepare myself to tell Sunshine the big news.

I am nervous, and I don't want him to reject us. I don't think he will, and I think he will be happy, which could bring us back together.

I hear the beep as he enters. I had a chip put in his wedding ring so he could stay here even when I was not around. That is just one sign of how much I am committed to him and how much I trust him.

As he enters, I say, "Welcome home, Sunshine. How was the mission?"

He waves to me with his left hand, but no ring is on his finger. That's odd.

"Hey R…Asia. It was fine; we took care of the drug problem and got all our money back and then some."

He pats me on the shoulder and sits on the couch.

Why is he acting like this?

Where's his ring?

Is this the end for us?

I clear my throat, "I made hamburgers for dinner. Are you hungry?"

His mouth turns upward in disgust, but he tries to fix it before I notice. "No thanks, Asia, I ate before I got here. We need to talk."

I shift where I am standing. "Yes, we do. Should I go first, or do you want to?"

He stands up, strokes my cheek, and pulls papers from his back pocket, "You're safe now. Our marriage is over."

What the fuck?

Is he serious?

Breathe, hear him out.

"You really want a divorce? Do you love me? Did you forget about the plans we made? What about having a family? What brought this on?"

He shrugged, "Those are the plans we made when we wanted to make our marriage work. I wanted a family with you at one point, but now I don't. You came back from the mission as a changed person. Who knows what you did on the mission? You probably slept with half of the crew, and that's not something that I can handle. I want someone who is committed to me and, no matter what stays faithful to me and our relationship. Plus, you poisoned them. How do I know you won't poison my food? Just sign the papers, please. Asia, I'm leaving you with two million dollars."

It's official, my heart broke in half.

"Where will you live, Sunshine?" I am holding back tears and keep stopping myself from putting my hand on my stomach.

He huffs, "I will go back to the compound. I don't mind living with my Bratva family."

Another stab in the heart, the men is still his family, but he's already cast me aside. "No, you won't. I will have my lawyer amend the agreement. You can have my fortress; you already have unlimited access. I will deactivate all my crystal keys. I have a place to go, and I'll be busy for months, so that's the best solution. I already have a bag packed. I will never come over uninvited. I will get the agreement signed and back to you in two weeks."

I kissed his cheek. "Never forget; karma will reign. I love you, Sunshine. Goodbye."

I grab my bag and don't look back.

He wants me gone.

That's what he'll get.

I didn't deserve this, but Karma has a plan.

I may be broken and pregnant, but I'm still strong.

XXVII

Kass

Months Later....

My brother is a dumbass!

He didn't even listen to what Asia had to say.

Asia gave M, and me access to her security cameras since Roe is living there.

I went back and watched the argument, the nerve of Roe to say the things that he did to Asia.

Asia had the lawyers fix the divorce agreement, showing Roe gets the house.

Asia decided she didn't want the big place anymore since it would just be her and the baby. I set her up in my old apartment so she still has plenty of space.

M was supposed to have the lawyer file the divorce papers months ago, but he didn't.

The lawyer has them, but they are not filed with the court.

M has decided that Roe and Asia belong together, so he will do anything in his power to keep them together, even if it means paying the lawyers more to not file them.

But as far as Asia and Roe know, they are divorced.

Asia has been staying at the apartments for eight and a half months now. She doesn't want to see Roe, so she avoids him like the plague.

Roe has been very attentive to my needs during my pregnancy. I wish he was like that with Asia. M has been making sure we are both fully taken care of.

M has been constantly dropping hints that Asia is pregnant, but it's like Roe doesn't care at all.

I have had a tough pregnancy.

I have been hospitalized twice now.

The first time was because I was having heart issues, and the second time was due to not being able to feel the baby move at all.

Asia has been there every step of the way, and I have not left her side either.

We are going to our traditional spa day today, as a last-moment experience before both babies arrive. I am having a little boy and Asia is having a little girl, so either way, my family is complete. The doctor said I may not survive the birth, and my body may not be ready for the pain in labor.

But I have accepted that fact and made the necessary arrangements to ensure my little M is taken care of.

I knock on Asia's door, and she answers.

We are off to the spa.

XXVIII

Red

I need to relax. This is the last spa day before our munchkins arrive.

We decided to walk to get our exercise in, especially since we are safe now.

Nothing has happened to us over these eight months.

I had a feeling someone was following us, but Massimo looked into it and couldn't find anything.

Walking makes us feel independent and strong, even at eight and a half months pregnant.

Before we get to the spa, we are stopped by an elderly lady. "Excuse me, dears. Can you please help me find my glasses? I lost them somewhere between here and the spa."

Okay, that's odd, but it's on our way so we can help her.

Kass answered, "Of course, we can help you let's look!"

We are looking for the glasses as we continue to walk.

I ask, "Where's the last spot you remember having them? What color are they?"

She stops walking to think, "The last time they were on my head was at the bookstore. They are black with red hearts on them."

"Okay, let's go check there." I reply.

We enter the bookstore; there they are sitting on the dollar book table.

She runs and grabs them, then returns to us and hugs us.

"Thank you so much! I hope I didn't take too much of your time!"

Kass chuckled, "It's no problem. Have a good day!"

We continued a short trek to the spa.

Suddenly, I feel a prick in my arm.

I don't see who it is before it goes black.

Well fuck.

I have done dangerous missions but I am taken down on a walk.

The last thing I hear is Kass scream, "Asia!"

XXIX

Kass

What just happened?

One minute, we are on the way to the spa; the next minute, I am waking up in an abandoned building.

Getting kidnapped eight and a half months pregnant is a nightmare.

I have to survive this!

Asia is still passed out on a moldy mattress on the other side of the room, and I woke up on one on the opposite side.

Our hands are bound, and there is a note at my feet that reads:

You both are ungrateful and don't know how to treat good men. Get comfortable; this is where you both die. Once you both are dead, Roman and Massimo will be mine.

~S

Part Three

XXX

Roman

I'm out with Massimo after working all day. We decided to go to Don's Diner so Kass wouldn't have to cook dinner. It was a slow night at Don's so we were in and out with ease.

I can tell Kass is ready for this pregnancy to be over. It takes all the energy she can muster to do little things like putting her shoes on.

She's afraid she won't make it through birth, but Massimo and I will not let anything happen to her.

Massimo has been acting very odd lately. He has been talking a lot more about Asia and how she is somehow struggling. That is my ex-wife. I shouldn't care what is going on with her, but I do. I care a lot.

I wanted to stay married to Asia, but I couldn't shake the feeling that something has changed.

As we return to Massimo's apartment, Jared is waiting outside the door.

"Jared, you never come inside. What is wrong?" Massimo jokes.

Jared sighs, "I am sorry, boss. They are both missing. They never came to meet me outside the spa. I called the spa, but they never made it to their appointment."

Massimo is enraged. I have never seen him this furious. "YOU'RE TELLING ME THAT TWO PREGNANT WOMEN ARE MISSING, AND I AM JUST NOW BEING INFORMED! GET THE RECON TEAM ON IT NOW! I WANT A UPDATE IN FIFTEEN MINUTES!"

Another code red!

What is going on in this world?

Wait, two pregnant women?

I retort, "Boss, my sister is missing. Who else is missing? Who else in our crew is pregnant?"

I see his eyes soften, "Your wife."

I cackle, "I don't have a wife, boss. I am divorced."

He pats my shoulder, "We never had the lawyer file the papers. We thought you would stop being an idiot and come to your senses! We saw the video of your and Asia's fight. That is what I have been hinting at. Kass and Asia are pregnant at the exact same time. They have been going to doctor appointments together since they found out. Asia knew you felt like she betrayed you, but she didn't. She even had a DNA test to see how close Kass DNA was to the baby; Roman, you are a father. She was trying to tell you the day you fought, but you told her you didn't want a family with her. Kass and I have been taking care of her and making sure she has an easy pregnancy. But now both our wives are missing, and they could go into labor at any second!"

What?

Red is pregnant?

How?

Am I going to be a father?

She was telling me the night we broke up?

I snap into protector mode, "Let's move! We have to get our women! We need to protect those babies!"

XXXI

Red

I am so tired of being kidnapped.

This is getting annoying.

I am very irritated as I wake up from whatever they used to knock me out.

When I snap out of it I see Kass, I automatically go into protection mode. "Kass! Are you okay? Do we know what's going on? Are you having any labor pains? Is munchkin kicking?"

She just looks at me with tears in her eyes and says, "This is where we die."

She hands me the note and unties my hands.

What the fuck!

Who wrote this?

Who is S?

XXXII

S

As I listen to these dumb women converse, I am trying to decide which one to kill first.

Should I kill Kass, the wife of the Don?

I could take her place and be a queen!

Or Asia, the pregnant spy who won't be missed?

Her ex-husband doesn't even miss her.

It will bring me great pleasure to kill these ungrateful women.

Massimo and Roe are powerful men who deserve a woman who can match them stride for stride.

I want to know what Massimo was thinking when he married Kass. What did she do to earn his love? She must have done something significant!

Who would willingly choose someone who is a hindrance?

Roman did the right thing by divorcing Asia. She looks high-maintenance.

She's the type to spend everyone else's money before even touching her own.

Roman deserves a woman who has her own income, and that will spoil him.

I know who I will kill first.

I prep my Glock.

They will not know what hit them.

She will die.

I deserve to be a queen.

XXXIII

Red

The medicine has entirely worn off now.

I am back to all my work and not playing Asia.

I will protect Kass with all my might.

I hear a cocking sound right outside the door.

As the doorknob turns, I rush to throw myself in front of Kass.

The door opens, and Sasha stands with a Glock pointed straight at Kass.

What the fuck?

She grins at me as I approach Kass, "Hello, sister. Are you ready to die?"

I am entirely defensive, "I am not your sister! What the hell do you think you're doing, Sasha? I got you out of the ring. What is the point of drugging and kidnapping us?"

She tisks, "The point is to eliminate you and Kass here and claim your men and babies as my own. You ungrateful women do not give Massimo and Roman the respect they deserve! I have been watching you both for months! Asia, I would never hide a baby from my partner, ex or not. And Kass, you are too fragile to stand beside a Don! Oh, and Asia, I recently discovered you are my sister in two ways. First, we have the same biological mother and father. Secondly, Shelia adopted us both. So I suffered for so many years because you ran away from Shelia! So, I will be doing myself and your men a service by killing you both! But I will start with little Miss Fragile."

Are you kidding? Is this psychopath really related to me?

She blames me for her hard life because I ran away. So that's her game: blaming everyone else for her wrongdoings.

I will play on that so she gets distracted and doesn't want to kill Kass.

I laugh, "Oh, you poor naive darling! Do you think I give a rat's ass about what you went through? You forget I was in your ungrateful shoes. Shelia made me who I am today by tormenting me every day of my existence with her. But she's the reason I rescue women from the ring, and no woman deserves to go through that pain and violation. Do you think we are ungrateful to our men? No, honey, they are ungrateful! I am richer than Roman; I even gave him my house during the divorce. And Kass killed the last woman who touched her man the wrong way. But you don't deserve the life we have. You blame everyone else for your problems. But in reality, you are to blame for all the negativity in your life, so this will always be your fate! You will always be the second best while we reign! I won't let you have our babies or our men."

I see wrath in her eyes, "Time for you to die, Asia. I will spoil your baby just enough for a few years before I kill it, too!"

Okay, she is a real dumb blonde!

"Kill me! It will only prove that you will always be second! Roman may not love me, but Kass and Massimo do. So good luck escaping their revenge!" I retort.

I approach Sasha, and she glares at me just like Dust did.

I am just in her way, and she needs to fix it.

I might actually die here.

XXXIV

Sasha

She will not speak to me like that!

I am better than her!

I don't run from situations; I embrace them!

Shelia made me into the perfect woman!

I can have any man I want, so I will have two instead of one!

She doesn't deserve to be a mother!

I would cherish the child and give it the best life possible until it asks about its real mother.

Then, I will end it and make it look like an accident.

I feel my hand tighten around my Glock, "Enjoy death while I enjoy your baby and your man! Don't worry, I won't shoot Kass. I will just cut her baby out of her after you are dead!"

XXXV

Red

I swiftly turn to Kass, "I love you! And you were right; I still love your brother! Take care of yourself and Roman. Don't let my baby suffer in her hands!"

My tears are falling like a waterfall.

After all the good I did, Karma has shown her face!

I must protect Kass!

I will die right now.

I will die in peace.

XXXVI

Kass

"No!"

I scream as the shot rings out!

Asia falls to her knees, clutching her belly.

She mouths, "I love you, sis."

She starts bleeding from the gunshot and between her legs at the same time.

I must act fast to save them both!

Asia's knife is sticking out of the top of her boot!

This is my chance!

I hurry over to Asia.

She is still breathing but barely.

I whisper, "I will save you both. You're not allowed to die on me."

I sneakily grab her knife and stand up to face Sasha.

"Are you ready to die now, Kass?" She asks.

I reply, "Are you ready, Sasha?"

She gasps, "You think a handicapped pregnant woman can kill me? You are out of your mind! You will suffer the same fate as Asia!"

She raises her Glock at me.

She has no idea who she is messing with!

I laugh at her, "I will always reign! Do you know why? It is because everyone has had the same opinion of me as you do. They look at me and think I am incapable of doing what they do. But in reality, they are incapable of being me!"

Before Sasha can even pull the trigger, I pull the knife from my back and throw it just as I have been training all my girls.

I throw the knife just like I would a dart, with full force.

Asia always keeps her knives sharp enough to pierce any body part.

The knife lands right where intended, straight in Sasha's heart.

She is stunned.

She clutches her chest as blood pours out of her chest and mouth.

She doesn't fight as I pull the knife from her chest.

"Remember Sasha, a handicapped pregnant lady killed you."

She tried to grip my neck, but I shooed her hand away.

"Never threaten my family. Karma is real."

BANG!

I AM KARMA!

XXXVII

Roman

BANG!

Who fired a shot?

We hear a piercing scream as we finally make it to Kass and Asia's location.

I automatically take off running!

It doesn't matter whose scream it was; we need to save them both!

I will not lose anyone today!

I bust through the basement door; Kass is clutching her stomach.

She notices me and screams, "SAVE HER NOW! SHE HAS BEEN BLEEDING OUT FOR THE LAST TEN MINUTES!"

That's when I see her in a pool of blood.

Kass takes a deep breath, "Massimo, my water broke. I am in labor. Please get me and Kass to the hospital! She can't die! She saved me. Sasha wanted me dead first! Please hurry!"

Kass is in labor, and Asia is bleeding out!

I jump into action!

Massimo is already carrying Kass out.

I call the clean-up crew to burn this place down.

I check Red's pulse; it is faint, but it's there.

I kiss her cheek, "Fight, Red! Fight!"

My tears coat her bloody body.

I carefully lift her into my arms and race out the door to catch up with Massimo.

I know she can't hear me, "I love you, don't leave me. I will cherish you both forever, live for us!"

My tears know no end.

We enter the car just as the clean-up crew arrives, and within seconds, the place is in flames.

Arson strikes again.

Jared races to the hospital; Massimo calls Doctor Sara.

She is waiting outside for us.

"Massimo, take Kassani to room 2A. Doctor Jan is waiting for you. Jan has delivered multiple babies where the mother has had CP. Kass is in the best of hands. We need to get Asia to the OR now, and we have to try to save them both!" Doctor Sara says.

Two nurses snatch Red from me.

I am left alone.

Massimo is making sure Kass and Munchkin have a safe delivery.

Asia is rushed to OR.

If I lose anyone today, I don't know what I will do.

I am not religious, but to whoever will listen, please save my family!

All of them, please don't let any of them die today.

XXXVIII

Kass

"AHHHHHHHH! WHY DID YOU DO THIS TO ME!"

I am screaming my head off as another contraction hits me.

M holds me, "Calm down, my love. It will be worth it once it is over. Push, breathe, and stay calm."

"I WILL KILL YOU! DO NOT TELL ME TO CALM DOWN! AHHHHHH!"

M kisses my forehead.

I love him, but this pain is immense!

My heart is beating out of my chest, my eyes want to close.

I hear Doctor Jan say, "Stay with me, Kassani! One more push!"

I push one more time, and I hear a small cry.

My heart is so whole.

Doctor Jan puts him on my chest. He has M's dark hair and my blue eyes.

He stops crying as his face touches mine.

My life is complete.

Just as they remove little M from my eyes close.

The last thing I hear is Doctor Jan scream, "CODE BLUE!"

The light is calling me...

XXXIX

Roman

I look at my watch again; two hours have lapsed, and I still haven't heard anything about Kass or Red.

A nurse motions for me as I run my fingers through my hair.

They lead me to the nursery.

There stands Massimo, looking through the window with tears flowing down his face.

He never cries.

"Boss, are you okay?" I ask.

He puts his hand on my shoulder, "Meet your nephew. Kass insisted he be named Warren Hart Ballentine."

I feel the tears forming again, "Boss, that's very sweet. I love the name."

Kass would always call me Warren when we were little.

I pat Massimo's shoulder. "He is adorable. How is Kass? Can I go see her?"

Massimo falls to the floor, crying, "They are still trying to revive her, she coded right after she held Warren. I can't lose her. I know you can't either. What did we do to deserve this?"

"NO! I CAN'T LOSE HER! TAKE ME TO HER!"

I collapse right next to him.

He replies, "They kicked me out of the room and told me to spend time with Warren so they could work on her."

Just as he lays his head in his hands, they tote another baby into the nursery, a little girl.

She looks like she has brown eyes and blonde hair.

The nurse approached us and crouched to our level.

"Gentlemen, we just brought baby girl Hart. You can see her right next to baby Ballentine. I am going to check on your wives now."

We both just nod, no words come to our lips.

We glance at each other and stand.

I look through the window and see Warren and Baby Hart sleeping peacefully.

Baby Hart is my little girl, and Red and I made her.

She is precious, peaceful, and lovable.

I am a father, and please let me be a brother and husband still.

XL

Red

29 days later.....

My body feels stale.

I can't move my feet. My body aches all over.

What am I waking up from?

What did Sasha do now?

There it is, the feeling that woke me up.

It feels like someone is constantly squeezing my right hand.

There we go, my eyes are opening.

I am greeted by an all-white room and the smell of rubbing alcohol.

Where am I? Am I in the hospital?

I look to my right, and Kass lies there looking at me.

"Good morning, sis." She smiles.

She woke me up, and she is still squeezing my hand.

"Kass, what happened? Are you okay? How's Munchkin?" I asked. My brain is working overtime to figure out why we are here.

Kass squeezes my hand again, "I woke up just before you did. I don't know much, but from the way my body feels, I would say something traumatic happened. But let's not jump to conclusions. I will page the doctor, and we will find out what's going on."

I nod.

Should I be alive?

Where's my baby?

What happened?

XLI

Roman

It's almost been a whole month that my sister and Red have been in a coma.

The doctors said they would both have the best chance of a full recovery if we allowed them to put them both in a medically induced coma.

Massimo and I have been leaning and learning on each other heavily.

Who knew parenthood could be so taxing and difficult?

Warren and Kassie are thriving.

Hailey and some of the other Bratva women have been helping out.

Keira has been video chatting with us every day. She and Marcus are planning to come back soon.

I need my wife. I know Massimo needs his, too.

Massimo has become the big brother I needed.

\I am thankful to call him family.

Without his strength and support, I would not have made it through this, both mentally and physically.

One day soon, we hope to return to some normality.

XLII

Red

We have been asleep for a month!

Are you kidding me?!

Kass and I have missed the first month of our babies' lives!

We will both have physical therapy for at least a month to relearn how to use our joints properly.

Kass called Jared and threatened him.

He will keep his mouth shut and come get us, not tell the men.

Remind me to stay on her good side.

XLIII

Roman

Massimo comes back inside from walking to the little market down the street.

His arms are full of bags.

He needed groceries, and both babies were sleeping, so I stayed to watch them while he ran errands.

He looks at me irritated, "Where the hell could Jared have run off to? I was going to get him to help bring the bags inside, but the car was not outside. He won't pick up the phone either."

I help take the bags and put the groceries away, "It's okay, boss. We got it under control."

He sighs, "I know, but I hoped to go to the hospital today. I need to check on our girls. I need an update. It feels like I am empty."

I just nod.

I have been empty since everything transpired.

I convinced myself that Red had cheated on me, but she didn't.

She was faithful to me and our marriage.

I will never forgive myself if I don't get to apologize to Red.

I want her to stay my wife so we can raise Kassie together.

Maybe we can see what Karma grants us.

XLIV

Kass

I hope my little M is okay.

I hope my big M is okay, too.

I hope Roman remained strong through all this.

He needs his chance to make things right with Asia.

Asia and I just want to get acquainted with everyday life again and watch our babies grow.

Asia deserves all the happiness in the world.

Let's hope Roe makes it right.

Roe deserves happiness, too.

Asia had given Roe a new hope—a hope of love, security, and partnership.

The ball is in his court; he better get it in the basket.

XLV

Red

With Jared supporting us, we make our way to Massimo's apartment.

Jared is very loyal.

He may look docile, but he is deadly.

He knows how much we appreciate him.

Jared was a Sergeant in the United States Army for ten years before he got out due to his wife's death.

He still wears his wedding ring. He is our secret weapon, he knows how to do things other people only dream about. He was the main reason Kass started training the girls.

We don't stop to knock; Kass uses her key card.

Moment of truth.

It's time to see my baby and my godchild.

Time to face Roman, am I ready?

No.

Can I forgive him?

I don't know.

Karma give me a sign.

XLVI

Roman

The babies woke up an hour ago.

Massimo is still on edge because Jared hasn't returned his call.

"Where could he be? He is a big, burly man, and he stands out. How come our recon team hasn't found him?"

A burly voice sounds from the doorway. "Because I am more scared of these two than you, boss."

Jared has Kass and Red on each arm.

Massimo runs to the door and sweeps Kass into his arms. "My love, you're here! How do you feel? I missed you. Come see Warren. You need to bond with him, but we will only handle what you can."

"Kass! I am so happy you're alive! Do what he says. We can't lose you! I love you, sis." Tears slide down my face.

I turn to speak to Red, and she is gone.

Massimo replies, "Jared texted. Asia was tired. At least that's what she said. She said she would come to meet the babies in the morning."

Kass gets out of Massimo's arms and smacks my shoulder. "You big dummy! You just messed up! She needed your affection! She was dreading coming home because she knew you would ignore her. I feel fine; we will watch the babies and call Hailey to help. You need to talk to her. Save your marriage. Get your happiness."

Kass hugs me and kisses my forehead.

I nod and head for the door.

I guess Karma sent Kass to whip me into shape, just like she has done all our lives.

This is my chance.

Karma, if you can hear me, please be on my side.

XLVII

Red

It's like he didn't even see me.

I know that's his sister, and he really missed her, but I felt like I was a waste of space.

Jared brought me to the apartment, making me miss my fortress now.

My heart needs a fortress.

I love him; he is the father of my child, but I can't stand to be in last place.

I have been in last place all my life, and I want to be at least second for once.

I lay on the bed, just wondering what my life could have been like if I had just rescued the girls and never fallen in love.

I am thankful for my little munchkin, but my heart hurts.

Just as I close my eyes, a voice sounds in the doorway.

"Red, you're mine. That will never change."

I sigh, "I was yours. Now I am mine and a baby girl's mother. You let me go, you divorced me. We are over, and there is no us. I will co-parent since I'm sure Massimo told you she is yours."

XLVIII

Roman

Tell her the truth!

Come clean!

I sit on the edge of the bed, "Red, just lay there and listen to me. I have a lot I need to say to you."

She looks at me with pain and regret and retorts, "Fine. But you only have ten minutes. I want to sleep."

I nod and take a deep, "Well, we are still legally married."

That makes her sit up and face me. "Massimo paid off the lawyer so he wouldn't have to file the papers with the court. So, after I tell you everything, if you want a legal divorce, Massimo will allow it. He just wants us to be happy there was no venom behind what he did. Our baby girl is perfect.

I named her Kassie because I know how important Kass is to us both. I was wrong for making assumptions about what happened on the mission, no okay, I was a real asshole. I am sorry, Red. You did not deserve to have my insecurities pushed on you. I know you didn't cheat on me. I had heard the stories of what you had to do on previous missions, and I was scared. I didn't realize how committed you were to me and our marriage. I love and appreciate you, and I am not afraid you will poison me. I know you have had to be strong and protect yourself all your life, but I am here now; that is my job. I will protect you and our little angel with all I have. We can make this marriage last and make it real! I do not want to co-parent. I want us to be a family. We both deserve happiness. This is Karma and Kass pushing us back together. So, Red, what do you say? Will you be my real wife?"

She just stares at me.

Does she understand?

Where do we stand?

Does she love me, or does she hate me?

Come on, Karma!

Give me a break!

XLIX

Red

Karma, what the fuck are doing?

I got my revenge on those who haunted me.

I did your will!

Why do you keep fucking with my mind like this?

Are we still married?

Is that a good thing or a bad thing?

His eyes radiate the truth.

But my heart is still unsure.

I take in his body language.

I analyze him from head to toe.

He remembered to take his shoes off.

That was very thoughtful of him—way to respect my pet peeves.

HE IS WEARING HIS WEDDING RING!

Why would he do that? Does he really still love me?

I need to stop staring at him like an idiot.

I look at the dresser, "Roman, why are you wearing your wedding ring?"

He whispers, "I have been wearing it since the day after our fight. I knew I messed up, and it didn't feel right not to have it on."

Wow, he looks like a man tormented.

Should I give him a chance?

Should I be the hardcore badass I am known to be?

Or should I be Red?

Who is Red?

That is a good question.

My eyes meet his, "Who is Red to you? Is she different than Asia?"

L

Roman

Why would she ask me that?

Is she doubting me that much?

I will fix her doubt.

I smile at her, "That's an easy question. First, yes, they are technically the same person. But Asia is who everyone gets to see. She can be nice or mean. It depends on the situation, but I know everyone only sees what you allow them to. Well, everyone but me. I get Red. Red is always honest. Red wears her heart on her sleeve. Red is both a color and an emotion. Red is obsessed with crystals and saving girls who get into bad situations. Red is passionate. Red gives Sunshine his brightness. Red is kinky and fun. Red can only be seen when Sunshine is around. So, without me, you are just Asia, but with me, you are Red. With me, you are loved."

Her doubt is fading from her eyes.

Her body is relaxing.

She looks like her faith in us is restored.

I hope Red will stay mine.

LI

Red

Does Sunshine think all that about me is true?

Red, to him, sounds impressive.

Can I live up to his expectations?

To him, I am his world.

So I am number one to someone.

He deserves his happiness.

Can I be his happiness?

I deserve happiness, too.

He will be happy with me.

I can give him the world. We already have our little moon.

As long as he stays honest with me, we can do this.

I know what I want.

I want him.

I want us.

I scoot towards him and caress his cheek.

He leans into my gesture.

"I want you, Sunshine. I want us. I will fight for you. You are the sun for our family, and Kassie is our moon. I will give you everything in between."

LII

Roman

She smiles her infectious smile, and she crawls in my lap.

Her nose touches mine, "I love you, Sunshine. I will love you forever and always."

Her body fits perfectly in mine. Red is what fairy-tales are made of; she was meant to be a princess. But not the damsel in distress kind, but the I can handle anything life throws at me kind.

She has escaped death many of times, but I will never put her in a situation like that again.

I kiss her lips, this kiss is a I missed you kiss.

A never leave me again kiss.

A you are mine kiss.

I press my lips to her neck and whisper, "I have two things that belong to you. Do you want them now or later?"

She moans, "Now."

I kiss a path from her neck to her ear, "The first thing I have for you is my heart; the day you give it back means we are done for good."

I take the new and improved crystal from my pocket.

It is a five-inch real crystal heart.

I also had it fitted with the chip to her fortress, but it is in the chain, so it doesn't damage the integrity of the crystal.

I fasten the gift around her neck.

Her reaction says it all, the tears of happiness following down her cheeks and her arms hugging my neck.

I then pull her custom wedding set from my shirt pocket, "Second, here is your wedding set back." I carefully slip it on her finger, "The same thing goes for this: you give it back to me, that will symbolize the end of us. Can you handle my terms, Red?"

She kisses me. Her kiss says, "Forever."

But her lips say, "Always."

LIII

Red

2 years later

I never expected that I would fall in love.

Two years later, I have everything any woman could dream of!

I have a loving husband and a beautiful daughter.

Kassie is fully wrapped around her daddy's finger, a pry bar couldn't even separate them.

Roe will set the bar high, no man is ever going to compare to her daddy.

She loves me just as much, but I am grateful for her bond with all the men in our family.

Nothing will ever happen to our little Kassie because they must get through the Ballentine Bratva.

One day, Kassie will learn how dangerous her mommy is, but we will keep that a secret for as long as possible.

Sunshine never lets me rest when it comes to his appetite.

We still find time to satisfy each other twice a day.

Vanilla is not in our vocabulary, but kinky is.

Never did I imagine I would find a man who could satisfy my appetite in the bedroom and my appetite in the kitchen as well.

I have started to feel weird again.

I am constantly hungry, and don't get me started on the smells!

I took a test this morning.

Baby Hart number two is on the way!

I can't wait until I can tell Kass!

My life has ultimately become the greatest reward I have ever received.

I guess it took Karma a while to total up all the good I have done and cancel out the bad I have repented for.

Roman

In the end, Red getting her revenge was the best thing that happened to me.

Yes, we almost gave up on our marriage.

Yes, Red almost died.

Yes, I was a dumbass; Kass reminds me every day.

But I have a loving wife and daughter, as well as a stronger bonded Bratva.

Will I let Kassie know about what we stand for and what we do? Maybe one day when she is older and more mature.

Would I let her date someone that is a part of this life? We would have to see; it would depend on many things.

But Kassie dating is a long time from now, as far as I am concerned men beware!

Nobody is good enough for my little Moon.

Jared

Seeing all this love around me makes me long for a partner.

My wife has been dead for four years now.

I glance at my wedding ring.

Her death forced me to retire from the Army.

I served ten years in the Army.

It was my life.

Maybe thats why Sharon died, she may have felt like my love for the Army was more then my love for her.

I may never know the answer, but I know that if love comes my way again I will not let it slip through my fingers.

THE END......FOR NOW!

IS LOVE MEANT TO BE FOR THIS VET, JARED?

CHECK OUT LOVE'S FREEDOM TO FIND OUT!

ALWAYS LET YOUR HEART BE YOUR GUIDING CRYSTAL!

About the Author

Summer N Dawn is a small-town woman, just trying to live her dream.

She has cerebral palsy but doesn't let that stop her.

Showing the world that dreams can come true at any point in life.

She creates worlds so everyone can find a place to fit in.

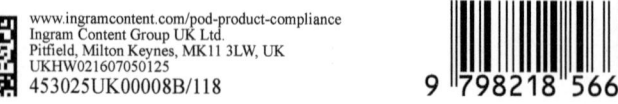